OLD AND NEW P

OLD AND NEW POVERTY

The Challenge for Reform

Edited by
Klaus Funken and Penny Cooper
for the Friedrich Ebert Foundation

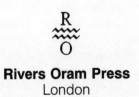

Rivers Oram Press
London

First published in 1995 by
Rivers Oram Press
144 Hemingford Road, London N1 1DE

Published in the USA by
Paul and Company
Post Office Box 442, Concord, MA 01742

Phototypeset in Sabon by Intype, London
and printed in Great Britain
by T.J. Press (Padstow) Ltd, Padstow, Cornwall

Designed by Lesley Stewart

British Library Cataloguing in Publication Data
A catalogue record for this book is available from the British Library

ISBN 1–85489–078–6
ISBN 1–85489–079–4 pbk

CONTENTS

LIST OF TABLES AND FIGURES

LIST OF CONTRIBUTORS

Roger Lawson is Senior Lecturer in Social Policy at the University of Southampton. He has taught at the Universities of Cardiff and Glasgow and has been Visiting Professor at the University of Frankfurt and Research Fellow at the Institute for International Social Law in Munich. He has published widely on social issues and social policies in Europe. He recently co-chaired (with William Julius Wilson) an international project on trends since the 1970s in poverty and social policy in Europe and North America. This research is published in *Poverty, Inequality and the Future of Social Policy* with Katherine McFate and W. J. Wilson (Russell Sage, 1995).

Ruth Lister is Professor of Social Policy at the University of Loughborough. She was Professor of Applied Social Studies at the University of Bradford and a former director of the Child Poverty Action Group. She has served on the Commission on Social Justice, the Opsahl Commission on the future of Northern Ireland and as Vice-Chair of the National Council for Voluntary Organisations. She has published widely on issues surrounding poverty, income maintenance and citizenship and is currently writing a book on women's citizenship.

Chris Pond is Director of the Low Pay Unit in London. A regular television and radio broadcaster, he has held academic and research positions at the Universities of Middlesex, Surrey, Kent, London and at the Open University. He has written widely on poverty and social policy and is currently writing a book on low pay in Britain.

An engineer, an economics graduate and former student of the Ecole Nationale d'Administration (ENA), **Michel Raymond** is General Inspector for Social Affairs at the French Ministry of Social

Affairs, where he was involved in drafting the 1988 law to set up the RMI (the minimum benefit paid to those with no other income). Since then he has been working on the implementation of the RMI and runs organisations in the social sector.

Until 1995, Dr **Bernd Schulte** was a Research Fellow at the Max-Planck-Institut für Ausländisches und Internationales Sozialrecht in Munich, specialising in Comparative Law, EC Law and Social Law. He is now Jean-Monnet Professor of Labour Relations, Social Policy and Social Law at the University of Bielefeld and has written widely on social policy in Germany and throughout the European Union.

Professor **Wolfgang Schütte** was born in 1947 and studied jurisprudence and education. Since 1984 he has been Professor of Social Legislation at the Fachhochschule in Hamburg. In 1995 he became the Chair of the founding commission of the study on care and health. He has written widely on education policy, socialisation, poverty development, social policy and social legislation.

Professor **Peter Townsend** is Emeritus Professor of Social Policy at the University of Bristol. After early years as Research Fellow and Lecturer at the LSE, he was appointed Professor of Sociology at the foundation of Essex University in 1963. In 1982 he moved to the University of Bristol as Professor of Social Policy. In 1991–2 he was the Michael Harrington Distinguished Visiting Professor of Social Science, Queens College, City University of New York. He has also contributed to Open University courses on elderly people, the family, health and disability. He is best known for his book *Poverty in the United Kingdom* (1979) and for his co-authorship of the Black Report, *Inequalities in Health* (1982). Recently he has worked for the ILO, the UNDP, the EU and the UN, concentrating on international social policy. His most recent work is *The International Analysis of Poverty* (1993). For over twenty years, Townsend was Chair of the Child Poverty Action Group and is now its President. He is the Chair of the Disability Alliance and has also served as President of the Psychiatric Rehabilitation Association and of MENCAP (South-West Region).

The Editors

Klaus Funken holds a doctorate in social sciences and has held academic posts in various German universities. He worked for the Social Democratic Party (SPD) Parliamentary Group in the German Bundestag before going to China as the director of China's Friedrich Ebert Foundation. From 1992 to 1995 he was director of the Foundation's London office and is once again working for the SPD at the Bundestag in Germany.

Penny Cooper is a research assistant at the Friedrich Ebert Foundation's London office.

PREFACE

This publication is largely based on the Friedrich Ebert Foundation Euroseminar: 'Old and New Poverty in the Welfare States, A Challenge to Reform our Social Security Systems?', which was held in December 1993.

The seminar was attended by poverty experts from all over Europe. The papers included here focus on European and worldwide experiences of poverty and fill an important gap in the current debate on poverty in our welfare states.

The Friedrich Ebert Foundation would like to take this opportunity to thank all the participants for making such a worthwhile contribution to this important debate.

Klaus Funken
Penny Cooper
London, 1995

INTRODUCTION

Klaus Funken

Poverty is one of the most underrated problems of our time. As our societies have become more and more affluent, the number of poor and needy people has continued to rise. Over the past twenty years economic growth in Germany has risen by over 70 per cent in real terms and the number of poor people has more than doubled in the same period. Over the last few decades, two-thirds of the German population have enjoyed untold wealth, the remaining one-third has been denied this wealth and is becoming more and more dependent on the welfare state.

This development is either sidestepped or completely ignored. Scientists argue about what poverty really is and how to define it. Politicians would rather close their eyes to the ravages of poverty all around them or pass the buck straight to the professional lobbyists, to whom it is just a job. And what about the man in the street? He stumbles over ragged bodies outside stylish shopping centres and is upset by the sight.

In almost every large industrial nation in the West, between 5 per cent and 10 per cent of the population have no access to its prosperity or wealth and have no prospect of ever being entitled to share in affluence. That is the core issue of the new poverty.

In some, albeit minority, sectors of the population in our industrial societies we are approaching poverty levels which are reminiscent of the Less Developed Countries – not just in relative terms, but in real terms as well.

Poverty no longer marks a temporary crisis point which can be overcome in time. Poverty is becoming more of an inevitably permanent state. This is the harrowing cost of rising long-term mass unemployment over the past twenty years.

The second generation is now growing up with unemployed parents and has experienced its inevitable social decline. This is where old poverty among the older generation of unemployed

1

meets new poverty among young people who are caught up in a vicious circle of unemployment and social deprivation.

The long-term unemployed have been particularly hard hit. Permanent exclusion from the job market has spawned a new type of 'chronic poverty', from which it is becoming more and more difficult to escape from continued unemployment, loss of self-respect, fear of failure, aggression, increasing violence and confrontational behaviour in the personal and social sphere, family breakdowns, extreme psychological instability, dependence on surrogates and ultimately drugs and crime. The poverty trap is a familiar, well-documented and researched subject. What is so shocking is that there is so little sense of responsibility among those in economic and political circles who could help.

Old poverty affected people left in dire straits who fell into difficulties through no fault of their own and slipped through the social net. Many are older people, particularly older women, who have not paid enough contributions and are only entitled to a paltry pension. Yet this problem has eased to some extent over the past decade. The number of old people living on social security has declined substantially. In the UK numbers fell by 25 per cent between 1974 and 1991. But the number of children under the age of sixteen who were dependent on social security over the same period has quadrupled.

New poverty affects young people who have never really had a chance in life. They mainly come from one-parent families and are left to fend for themselves. The majority leaves school without any qualifications and can't find work. First, young people end up in the so-called 'alternative job market' doing part-time work and then they drift into black market work and finally turn their backs on work permanently. Many end up taking drugs because they are desperate, bored and frustrated.

New-age poverty affects entire sectors of the population. These people are victims of racial discrimination, black people in the States, Arabs in France, Asians and black people in the UK and Turks in Germany. The nightmare scenario of new-age poverty in minority groups is already unfolding before in the US inner cities. Now, thirty years after the civil rights movement, most black people in urban locations have fewer prospects than ever. William Julius Wilson writes, 'Even the most pessimistic observers of urban life in America during the riots of the 1960s hardly anticipated the dramatic increases of social dislocation . . . and the growing social

problems – joblessness, family disruption, teenage pregnancy, failing schools, crime and drugs – that involve many of those who live
in the inner city'. It is hardly surprising that more black people
than ever are serving prison sentences for crimes. The proportion
of blacks among the prison population is higher and there are
currently more black people in prison than at university or college.

The most frightening aspect is the apathy, the way this trend
is shrugged off and accepted by most people. The Conservative
revolutions in the US and the UK were just beginning to create a
stir when the first waves of mass unemployment hit in the 1970s
and severely overburdened the welfare system. Yet, instead of being
reinforced the system has been systematically torn apart. Instead
of gearing up the welfare state for the new challenges of the global
economy, it is being dismantled. Instead of combatting poverty by
addressing the root problem, i.e. mass unemployment, job markets
are being equated with product and capital markets with devastat-
ing results for those in marginal jobs. Now, all those who cannot
meet the short-term profitability targets set by the bosses are being
catapulted out of the job market.

The Conservatives have managed to convince the public of the
importance of shifting the blame. This has severe repercussions. It
is the poor, unemployed dropouts, single parents, blacks, Indians,
Turks and Arabs who are forced to justify how they came to be in
such desperate straits. Blaming the victims has become a cheap
Conservative cliché. In addition to the funding crisis surrounding
the welfare state, there is now a legitimacy crisis which will be far
more harmful in the long term. Aid for the poorest is criticised more
than any other form of government expenditure. In a bid to attract
votes, politicians and even heads of government are free to call
the homeless, lone parents, the unemployed and racial minorities,
the'underclass', without fear of retribution. However, it would be
unfair to blame ideological rhetoric by individual party leaders or
the media, or lack of moral fibre for the success of the Conservative
roll-back policies. The Reaganites and Thatcherites do echo a desire
among the electorate to dismantle social cohesion within their
societies and leave the poor to their own fate. No party which
wants to win an election can resist the temptation. It is therefore
virtually impossible openly to discuss funding allocations and poverty action campaigns in our society in politics today. The word
'solidarity' has been given a bad name and has virtually disap-
peared from our vocabulary.

This new majority public view clearly represents a huge threat to the left-wing parties in Europe. Social Democratic parties fear internal rifts and often gloss this over with set compromises. Even Christian Democratic parties are having problems meeting the expectations of a fun-loving, egocentric electorate.

So there is no future for the poor and, as matters stand, their situation could worsen. Nation states are expected to lose more autonomy and political sovereignty within the borderless world of the twenty-first century. Less well qualified workers, particularly those in the manufacturing and service sectors, will be competing with Asia, Africa and Latin-America for global markets with the same machines and skills but for 100th of the average European wage. The industrialised West is facing untold pressure to realign costs and workers will be the victims.

1 THE CHALLENGE OF 'NEW POVERTY': LESSONS FROM EUROPE AND NORTH AMERICA

Roger Lawson

This paper draws upon evidence from Western Europe and North America to illustrate how the period since the late 1970s marks a watershed in 'First World' poverty and inequality. In contrast to the trends of the earlier post-war years, poverty rates have been rising on both sides of the Atlantic. At the same time, a variety of economic, social and political forces have been producing powerful new configurations of inequality and social closure. Described as 'the new poverty', these recent forms of inequality involve import-ant changes in the composition of economically marginal groups, the crystallisation of racial and ethnic divisions among them, a downward turn in their life chances, and an increase in their social and political isolation.

The growth of 'new poverty' is in part a consequence of the rolling back of social programmes and the more general erosion of the protective systems of social and economic co-operation erec-ted in the earlier post-war era. However, it also reflects new lines of social cleavage that have been emerging in Western societies in the wake of profound industrial change and of forces that have weakened and fragmented older social and family structures and traditional forms of solidarity. For a broad middle mass of society, including many skilled and affluent workers as well as the more conventional middle class, these forces have brought more open-ness and flexibility in economic and social relations. Opportunities have widened, as the traditional constraints of class, gender and ethnicity have waned in the middle and upper ranks of society, and as scope has been offered for more 'personalised' life styles.

By contrast, the trends in society below the middle mass have been pulling in the opposite direction. Here, national economic restructuring has left a large proportion of working-age citizens, including many younger people, unemployed, underemployed and socially and economically insecure. For many, the reality of the new post-industrial order is not merely more exposure than previously to the vagaries of the labour market but the fact, as the French sociologist André Gorz has put it, that they are 'threatened by loss of status and esteem, threatened by the contempt of others, by social exclusion'.[1] For an increasingly vulnerable minority, the prospects are a life more or less detached from the broader economic and social experiences of mainstream society. Economic insecurity has restricted opportunities in numerous other ways. It has increased the risks of family breakdown, reinforced gender inequalities, led to more hostile and fearful relationships in local communities, and – the most disturbing of recent trends – has hardened racial cleavages and fed new forms of xenophobia and racism among the less privileged.

The growth of First World poverty

In exploring these issues, it is important first of all to identify the main changes that have occurred in the incidence of First World poverty. The general upward thrust of poverty rates is now well documented, though good comparative data are available only for the first half of the period since the mid-1970s. Some of the most systematic estimates of the numbers of poor people in Western Europe are provided in a study prepared for the European Commission.[2] Using data from national income and expenditure surveys, the study defined as poor, or economically marginal, households with a disposable income of less than 50 per cent of the average disposable income in each country. Its findings suggested that in the 12 countries of the European Union, the number of people in poverty increased slightly between 1975 and 1980, from about 38.6 million to 39.5 million, but then jumped to approximately 43.9 million in 1985. Over the ten years, this involved a rise in the proportion of the population in poverty from 12.8 to 13.9 per cent. A recent rougher estimate by the European Commission suggests that by the early 1990s, in a community including the former East Germany, the number of people below the 50 per cent poverty line had jumped again to some 50 million.[3]

Figure 1.1 contains data from another research project that has taken a broader comparative view of 'new poverty'. Conducted

(a) Households with less than 50 per cent of median household income

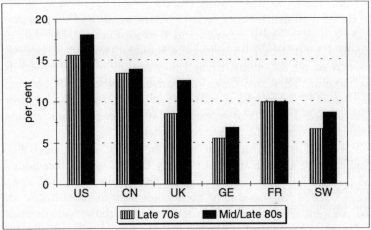

(b) Households with less than 40 per cent of median household income

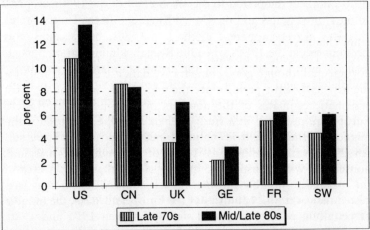

Notes: Periods 1 and 2 are: United States, 1979, 1986; Canada, 1981, 1987; United Kingdom, 1979, 1986; West Germany, 1981, 1984; France, 1979, 1984; Sweden, 1981, 1987

Source: Katherine McFate, Timothy Smeeding, Lee Rainwater, 'Markets and States: Income Trends and Transfer System Effectiveness in the 1980s' in McFate, Katherine, Roger Lawson and William Julius Wilson (eds) (1995) *Poverty, Inequality and the Future of Social Policy*

Figure 1.1 Poverty rates with heads aged 20–55, late-1970s and mid-1980s

under the auspices of the Joint Center for Political and Economic Studies (JCPES) in Washington, DC, the project has made a number of detailed comparisons of recent poverty trends and their under-lying causes in North America and Western Europe.[4] The data in figure 1.1 are based on a broadly similar definition of poverty to that of the EC study, though they are limited to non-elderly households. They also make comparisons of the trends between the late 1970s and the second half of the 1980s, using a more severe yardstick of relative poverty (40 per cent of households' income) as well as the 50 per cent measure.

As well as confirming the trends in the EC study, the JCPES findings give an indication of the way the tail of the distribution of poverty has been lengthening. In the countries shown, apart from Canada, the number of households with incomes below the 40 per cent level grew at a faster rate than those with incomes below the 50 per cent level. More striking, however, is the evidence that the most severe consequences of the social and economic dislocations in the period to the second half of the 1980s occurred in the United States and the United Kingdom. In the United States, this was already apparent in the late 1970s, but became more pronounced in the 1980s when the Reagan administration pursued policies aimed at improving the living standards of the broad middle class and relied on economic growth to trickle down and take care of the problems of the poor. Although the United States experienced more steady growth and lower unemployment than most of Europe in this period, the American poverty rate among the non-elderly population rose to more than double that of most European countries, and to almost three times the level in West Germany. By the second half of the 1980s, almost 1 in 5 non-elderly households in the United States fell below the 50 per cent poverty line.

Even more significant in this period was the changing depth or severity of poverty in the United States and the sharply divergent patterns of poverty concentration between racial minorities and whites. An indication of this is provided in data published by the United States Census Bureau. In recent years it has established a 'poorest of the poor' category, consisting of individuals whose annual income falls at least 50 per cent below the officially desig-nated poverty line. In 1975, 30 per cent of all the poor had incomes below 50 per cent of the poverty level. In 1988, 40 per cent did so. Among blacks, the increase was much sharper, from 32 per cent in 1975 to 48 per cent in 1988.[5]

In both the EC and JCPES studies, the United Kingdom has the distinction of having experienced the sharpest increases in poverty and income inequality in the 1980s. While this was more directly related than in the United States to the return of mass unemployment, it clearly reflected the close links between ideologies and economic and social strategies under Thatcher and Reagan. Indeed, what also characterises Britain's experience in the 1980s is the shift in the configuration of poverty and inequality away from a pattern associated with the European welfare states towards a North American pattern. This, in turn, was accompanied by a distinct change in poverty agendas that was well summed up by one of Mrs Thatcher's close advisers, David Willetts. Writing in 1988, he argued that British policies involved a shifting of the terms of the poverty and social security debates 'away from the tired old agenda of integrating tax and benefits and towards the new American agenda, where the real world questions of welfare dependency, and how much it is right to spend on the poor, figure prominently'.[6]

Other recently published data reveal how these trends persisted after the mid-1980s. Between 1979 and 1989, the number of Britons living in households with incomes on or below the minimum social assistance standards (Supplementary Benefit/Income Support) rose from 7.74 million to 11.33 million.[7] At the same time, because minimum benefits were not increased in line with average earnings, the standard of living of people on low incomes fell compared with the rest of the population.[8] An idea of the extent of the fall is given in figure 1.2, which is based on government statistics showing how the gap between the rich and poor grew rapidly in the 1980s. Between 1979 and 1990/1 the average real income of the bottom tenth of households (after housing costs) fell by 14 per cent, whereas the richest tenth experienced a 50 per cent increase. Overall, average household incomes rose in real terms by 36 per cent.

Compared with Britain and the United States, countries like Germany, France, the Netherlands and Sweden appear to have shown more capacity and willingness in the 1980s to mediate the effects of rapid economic and social change. Nevertheless, there is plenty of evidence of a clear reversal of the more egalitarian trends of the earlier post-war period. One illustration is to be found in

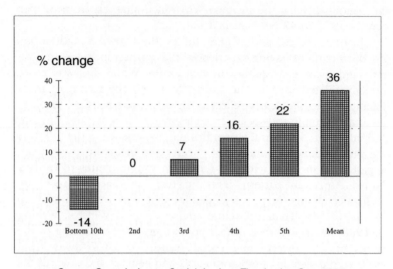

Source: Commission on Social Justice, *The Justice Gap*, 1993

Figure 1.2 United Kingdom: Change in Real Income of Bottom Half of Population, 1979–1990/1

the development of means-tested social assistance, the modernised version of traditional poor relief. A feature of most European welfare states between the 1940s and 1970s is the way they deliberately sought to make the need for this kind of assistance marginal and in turn to avoid the creation of a distinctive American-style 'welfare class'. This was, in a sense, a cornerstone of the European conception of social citizenship. It was given expression in a commitment both to full employment and to the steady enlargement of entitlements to universal social programmes, many of which were premised on assumptions of regular and stable employment. With this commitment, expenditures on means-tested assistance in the Scandinavian countries, Germany and the Netherlands fell from around 13 per cent of total social security expenditures in 1950 to roughly 2 per cent on the eve of the first Oil Crisis in 1973/4.[9]

The story of the mid-1970s to the mid-1990s is very different. Since the 1970s, European workers, especially those with low status and skills who have been vulnerable to unemployment, have found their rights to social insurance-based benefits steadily eroded. At the same time, all countries have experienced a substantial growth in households, such as lone-parent households, not easily accommodated by conventional social insurance measures. The consequences are readily apparent in the social assistance statistics which reveal significant increases both in expenditures and beneficiaries.[10] Belgium, for example, has seen a fivefold increase in the numbers receiving this relief since the 1970s.

In Germany, two decades ago, the idea of applying for regular 'subsistence aid' from the local *Sozialamt* was anathema to most workers, because of the stigma and feelings of shame attached to this kind of relief. In 1970, fewer than 700,000 people received regular weekly assistance, and over 40 per cent were elderly people, mostly elderly widows. By 1991, the numbers had risen to 3.1 million, only 300,000 of whom were in the new East German Länder, and an additional 1.1 million received other 'social assistance' such as medical aid. In 1991 the elderly accounted for only 16 per cent of the total of 4.2 million. Moreover, recent German studies suggest that a further 2–3 million people live in families eligible to receive assistance, but not applying because of lack of information and the sense of shame.[11] Significantly, too, as in Britain, these trends have occurred at a time when the standard of living of social assistance recipients has declined relative to the rest of the population. Between 1972 and 1991, the per capita real disposable income of households of wage and salary earners and pensioners increased by 90 per cent. For social assistance beneficiaries, by contrast, the rise was 36 per cent.[12]

In Continental Europe, there are also signs that the 1990s are witnessing a more marked acceleration of poverty and social polarisation than was evident in the 1980s. A feature of the 1990s recession is the sharp rise in long-term unemployment. In 1993, those unemployed for more than a year constituted about half of all the Western European unemployed, compared to 10 to 20 per cent in the rest of the industrialised world. Moreover, throughout Europe efforts to cut social expenditures have not only intensified in the 1990s but have occurred in a climate seemingly more hostile to the poor, or at least to certain sections of the poor such as lone parents, some of the unemployed, and foreign workers and asylum seekers. In Germany, for instance, critics of the much-heralded Solidarity Pact of 1993, aimed at diverting resources to the eastern Länder, have dubbed it 'a solidarity pact against the weak'. More than 80 per cent of the projected savings in social benefits are made up by cuts in benefits to the unemployed and in means-tested social assistance.[13] They include substantial cuts in benefits paid to asylum seekers and refugees.

The new poor

Poverty rates have not only been rising in most Western societies, they have grown disproportionately among the younger sections of society and the prime-age workforce. Indeed, a major feature of the 'new poverty' of the 1980s and 1990s is the increasing vulnerability of children and of young people denied access to the labour force. According to the JCPES study, the sharpest rises in First World poverty have occurred in child poverty, particularly in the English-speaking world. A Unicef report also draws attention to a 'weak and eroding commitment to children' in countries like Britain, the United States, Canada and Australia.[14] The report suggests that the condition of children declined most sharply during the 1980s in the United States, with the proportion of children living in families with less than 40 per cent of median disposable income rising to more than one in five. Britain, Canada and Australia each had roughly 10 per cent of children living below this poverty line.

That these trends are by no means confined to the English-speaking world is illustrated in figure 1.3. These contain comparisons by age of the number of people living in families receiving social assistance in the United Kingdom and Germany in the mid-1970s and in 1991. The British data confirm the observations above. While the number of elderly people relying on assistance fell from 1.8 million in 1974 to 1.4 million in 1991, the number of children under 16 rose from 800,00 to 2.3 million. In Germany the trends differ somewhat, with the sharpest increases occurring in the middle age ranges. Nevertheless, the growing proportion of children and young people among the 'welfare poor' is striking: there was almost a threefold increase among the under 15s and a fourfold increase in the 15–24 age group. German statistics, like the British, reveal also a steady lengthening of the period families have been relying on relief.

In interpreting data like this, it is important not to be misled by the trends among the elderly. On both sides of the Atlantic, statistics for the over-65s point to a substantial decline in the risk of poverty, but such figures hide widening disparities of income and welfare in the older population. In most countries differences

(a) Great Britain, 1974 and 1991, Recipients of Supplementary
Benefits (1974) and Income Support (1991)

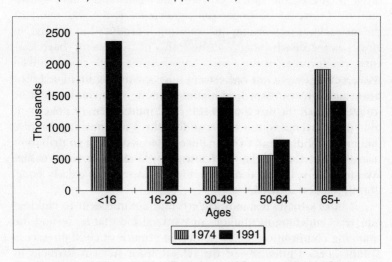

(b) Germany 1975 and 1991: Recipients of Regular Weekly Cash
Assistance

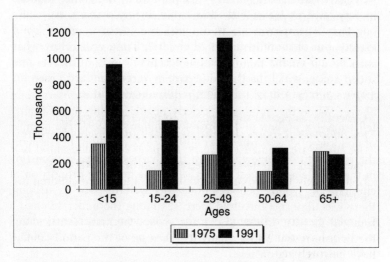

Sources: Great Britain: Department of Health and Social Security, *Social
Security Statistics*, 1975; Department of Social Security, *Statistics*, 1992;
Germany: Statistisches Bundesamt, *Sozialhife*, 1976 and 1993

Figure 1.3 Social Assistance Beneficiaries and Dependents by Age
Group in Great Britain and Germany (West), Mid-1970s and 1991

between the financial circumstances of younger pensioners and those of the oldest and most vulnerable pensioners have grown recently. However, of longer run significance is the way many of the inequalities of working life are being reproduced in old age. In effect, as the disadvantages of the status of 'retirement' have lessened, the fortunes of the elderly have become more closely linked with occupational class and esteem during working life. For Europeans and Americans with a lifetime of low wage employment or irregular work records there is still a substantial risk of poverty in old age, and there is little evidence that this is diminishing. Indeed, there is every prospect that the interrupted work and contribution records of today's long-term unemployed and growing casual labour force will turn them into a 'new class of the elderly poor' during the coming decades.

It is, of course, not only an 'eroding' commitment to children but these widening inequalities of working life that lie behind the changing composition of the poor. The growth of child poverty is a consequence primarily of the retreat from full employment in Western societies and the exposure of low income households to the vagaries and more pervasive inequalities of the labour market. Poverty research leaves little doubt that unemployment, especially long-term unemployment, is not just the major cause of child poverty, but of more instances of children living well below what many would regard as a minimum acceptable way of life. As one British study, which used a subjective poverty standard based on people's perceptions of minimum requirements, put it:

> Generally, as people slip deeper into poverty, the spectre of *unemployment* looms. In nearly one half of households where the adults are in intense poverty, the head of the household is unemployed. The effects of the recession of the 1980s have been sharply to increase the numbers of adults and children in intense poverty.[15]

A similar picture is painted by other European researchers, many of whom have tended to equate the 'new poverty' with the plight of the unemployed.[16]

While unemployment remains the major cause of poverty in the 1990s, there is also growing evidence that being in work is less likely to lift people out of poverty than was the case twenty years ago. This at least appears true of Europe. In the United States, the notion of the 'working poor' has long been built into the economy and society, to a far greater extent than in Europe. Over the past decade, however, increasing numbers of European workers have found themselves in the 'secondary labour market' with low wages and low skills, poor working conditions, weak trade union protection and a high risk of unemployment. Many are on temporary or part-time contracts, or in the grey areas of employment where employers can evade social and labour laws. This is not a minor phenomenon. In Britain, for example, by the end of the 1980s, more than a quarter of the male workforce were not in full-time, regular employment, while over 45 per cent of working women were part-time employees. In West Germany, by 1986 over a quarter of all workers were on fixed-term, part-time contracts. In the 1980s, half or more of all new employment created in France, Germany, the Netherlands and Spain consisted of workers on temporary contracts. As Standing (1995) has argued, the irony is that this casualisation of the lower segments of the workforce occurred at a point when 'the most vulnerable groups of all – ethnic minorities, women, migrants – were gaining some access to mainstream entitlements. The mainstream went backwards, leaving many more insecure, in numerous ways.'

Another example of the way labour market changes have been creating new cleavages between the 'mainstream' and those below is provided in a European Commission study of occupational segregation of men and women. It shows how, during the 1980s, 'professional jobs have become more open to well qualified women applicants throughout the Community, thereby reducing the domination of men at the middle and upper ends of the labour market'. Significantly, however, the study found the very opposite trends occurring among the many women in Europe who have moved into lower level clerical and service work and into production work in the 1980s. While job opportunities appeared to be opening up at one end of the spectrum, this other end had witnessed more closure, as male manual jobs, both skilled and unskilled, had remained relatively impervious to the influx of women in the workforce. The result over the decade, and for the female workforce as a whole, was a reinforcement of gender segregation and a perpetuation of male and female inequalities in terms of conditions and pay. As the study emphasises, this has had profound financial and social consequences for lower income households.

Among those most affected by these developments have been the growing numbers of working mothers from lone-parent households, many of whom are to be found working in the more segregated sections of the workforce. In the countries covered by the JCPES study, with the exception of Sweden, female-headed households were much more likely to be poor than couple-headed families. However, the degree of difference was by no means related to the extent to which mothers were able to enter paid employment. Britain's arrangements, under which most lone parents received state income support without having actively to seek employment, appeared more effective in limiting lone poverty than the German situation where there is more of an expectation that lone mothers should work. Occupational segregation and wage discrimination leave German women with incomes significantly lower than men, while family responsibilities (in a country where the formal school-day ends around 1 p.m.) keep many mothers in part-time work. But even when a woman works full-time, there is no guarantee that she will earn a family wage. In fact, over 15 per cent of full-time working mothers in the United States and almost 12 per cent of full-time working mothers in Canada failed to earn enough to keep themselves and their children out of poverty *even with* government assistance.

The sharp rise in female-headed families raises other questions, particularly about causes. In Britain, which now has a higher proportion of lone-parent families than other countries in the European Union, recent explanations of the rise have leaned heavily on the views of American conservative theorists, such as Charles Murray, who have focused on moral decline and on the incentives that welfare programmes provide. The issues are too complex to examine here. However, it should be noted that some of the most sophisticated empirical research on the subject, conducted in America in response to Murray's claims, has proven the welfare hypothesis unfruitful. Moreover, the research provides consistent evidence linking male economic status to family stability. In various historical and ethnographic studies as well as detailed analyses of survey data, male joblessness is identified as one of the most critical factors behind changing family structures.[19]

Race, ethnicity and poverty

Some of the most challenging and disturbing aspects of 'the new poverty' concern the links between race and poverty. There is much evidence on both sides of the Atlantic that the period since the 1970s has seen a hardening of racial and ethnic cleavages among the more disadvantaged segments of the population, while at the same time an opening up of opportunities for the more affluent and privileged among minorities. In the United States, where these trends are most pronounced, the prime beneficiaries of the civil rights era and of the affirmative action programmes that emerged in the 1970s have been the black professional classes and the upper fraction of the black labour force. In terms of absolute income, these groups have experienced a real advance over the past two decades, so much so that among those who have graduated from college and who are under 35 there are now virtually no differences in family incomes between black and white households. However, in a number of respects, the fate of millions of blacks concentrated in America's inner-city ghettos has been regression, not progress. As Wilson has argued:

> Even the most pessimistic observers of urban life in America during the ghetto riots of the 1960s hardly anticipated the dramatic increases in rates of social dislocation . . . [and] the growing social problems – joblessness, family disruption, teenage pregnancy, failing schools, crime and drugs – that involve many of those who live in the inner city.[20]

These trends pulling in opposite directions are readily apparent in recent American analyses of poverty and income inequality. The picture that emerges from poverty surveys covering the period between the 1960s and late 1980s is of some lessening in gender inequalities among the poor but a widening of differences between blacks and whites, especially among younger people of working age.[21] The racial divide is starkly portrayed in figure 1.4 which shows income distributions in the United States. When the distributions are pulled apart on racial lines, what looks like an inverted pyramid among whites becomes a regular pyramid among blacks. The figure brings out clearly the contrasting fortunes of the black elite and black poor between 1970s and 1990.

A startling illustration of one of the outcomes of these trends is provided by Troy Duster (1995) in a discussion of 'incarceration versus matriculation' in the United States. In 1986–8, 4.5 million white males were in higher education compared with 330,000 in prisons and jails, a ratio of more than 10 to 1. Among black males *more* were incarcerated (342,000) than were attending colleges and

White families 1970

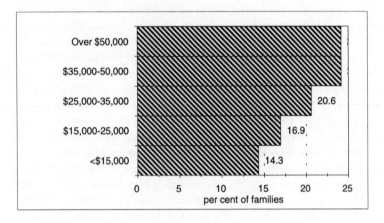

White Families 1990

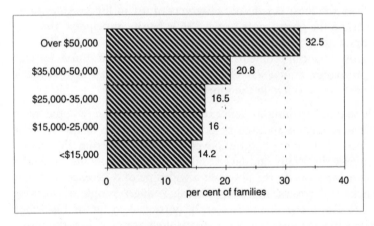

Source: Andrew Hacker (1992) *Two Nations, Black and White: Separate, Hostile and Unequal*

Figure 1.4   Income Distribution of Whites and Blacks in the USA

universities on a full-time basis (270,000). The proportion of the black population incarcerated was seven times that of whites, whereas in the 1950s the ratio was approximately four times. As Duster shows, it is the last two decades that have 'witnessed the greatest shift in the racial composition of prison inmates in US history'.[22]

Black families 1970

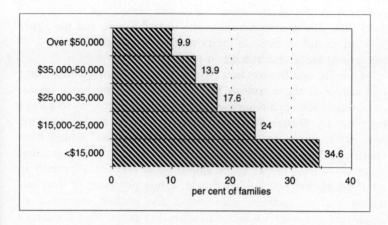

Black Families 1990

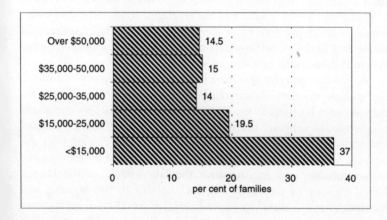

Duster's work also points to some of the new barriers to black progress that have served to offset apparent advances in political, civil and social rights. In education, for instance, the decades since the civil rights era have witnessed major changes in secondary school enrolment, and today black and white enrolment levels are virtually identical. In practice, however, this has been accompanied by a steady abandonment by whites of the public school sector, especially in central city areas. Today, one white child in four aged 4–15 attends a private school in the United States, and the figure is closer to one in three in urban centres. By contrast, around 90 per cent of black children are in public schools.

Of more significance, however, particularly from a comparative perspective, is the mounting US evidence of a resurgence of discrimination accompanying the shift from manufacturing to service employment. Duster draws on a wide range of studies showing how, while in the manufacturing sector blacks and whites have about equal success in obtaining jobs, whites are up to four times more likely than blacks to be employed in services, especially in retail establishments. Behind this lie subtle processes of discrimination and competition that reflect the greater sensitivity of employers in the service sector to what they perceive as a worker's 'presentation of self' and way of relating to customers, clients and the general public. Young people generally have been affected by these trends, but African American and Hispanic youth have been most vulnerable, and the most likely to be unemployed or to resort to the emerging alternative and underground economies. As Duster argues, one of the lessons in this for Europe is that 'Africans in Rome and Turks in Berlin will both experience these developments before Italian youth or German youth'.

In Europe, poverty literature has been remarkably colour-blind, and meaningful data identifying long-run trends are far more difficult to come by than in the United States. Nevertheless, the available evidence suggests that links between race or minority status and social exclusion and deprivation have been growing over the past two decades, and are now being compounded by the upsurge of xenophobia and racism since the late 1980s. In the United Kingdom, one of the most detailed analyses of the housing and location of ethnic minorities concludes that 'residential segregation in Britain is becoming more, not less, potent, as the twentieth century draws to a close'.[23] The study shows how initially, when the first post-war immigrants arrived in Britain, patterns of segregation tended to reflect the distribution of labour demand and the location of cheap housing. Subsequently, however, particularly as economic conditions worsened, segregation became an expression of more deeply entrenched racial inequalities and pressures that marginalised minorities, politically as well as socially.

Other British studies have addressed the issue of poverty more directly, though without adequate national statistics, they have drawn mainly upon local surveys and workforce and unemployment trends. Their broad conclusions are well summarised in a paper prepared for the Runnymede Trust:

> It is clear that there has been an increased racialisation of poverty: blackness and poverty are more correlated than they were some years ago. In spite of government concern with racial disadvantage, and the undoubted limited success of positive action and equal opportunity policies in helping to create a black middle class, the conditions of the black poor are deteriorating. Moreover the situation is being exacerbated by government policies intended to reduce welfare spending on social security and housing.[24]

In Continental Europe, the recessions of the 1980s and 1990s have underlined the particular vulnerability of immigrant and minority communities to economic stagnation, industrial restructuring and the decline of traditional manufacturing. Immigrant unemployment rates are commonly more than double those of the indigenous workforce, reaching levels ranging from 25 to 50 per cent in cities that have experienced unprecedented high levels of unemployment overall. Even in the Netherlands, with its comparatively good record of race relations, unemployment rates among Turks and North Africans rose during the 1980s to more than three times the levels of the native Dutch, while the Moluccan rates were almost four times higher. [25] There is evidence in the Netherlands that the rise in long-term joblessness among the minorities has led to sharply decreasing contacts with conventional groups and institutions in the larger society, despite the fact that a strong official regulation of the housing market has led to less overt discrimination and segregation in housing than in some other countries.[26] As elsewhere, too, many of those most acutely affected by these trends have been the second and third generation of minority youths who 'often suffer from educational deficiencies, are unable to find meaningful employment and are culturally and institutionally removed from the societies of their parents. Their isolation, dislocation and alienation have been increasing.'[27]

The situation in Germany provides, however, the most striking European example of the changing circumstances of minorities. Around 8 per cent of German population – over 6 million persons – are people of non-German origin, and mostly of non-German

(a) Numbers of Foreign Residents and Foreign Workers in Germany (West), 1967–1991

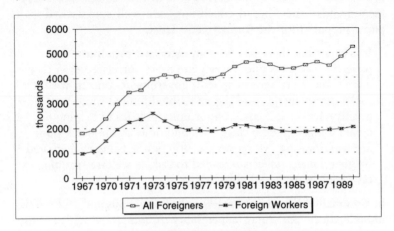

(b) Unemployment Rates of Germans (West) and Foreign Workers, 1966–1993

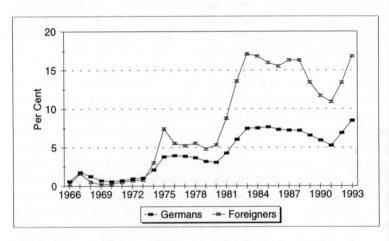

Sources: Amtliche Nachrichten der Bundesanstalt für Arbeit; Stastistiches Bundesamt, *Sozialhilfe*, 1993

Figure 1.5 Germany's Foreigners 1970s–1990s

citizenship, who are resident or have settled in the Federal Republic as a result of migration since the late 1950s. They include recent asylum seekers and refugees but the great majority consist of the

(c) Social Assistance Beneficiaries: Germans and Foreigners

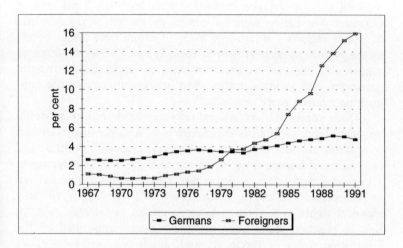

foreign workers and their families initially recruited during the classic *guestworker* era in the 1960s and early 1970s. A key assumption of that era, which crucially limited foreigners' rights and efforts to integrate them, was that their recruitment was a temporary expedient. It was necessary to overcome certain short- and medium-term labour requirements in the German economy, particularly in sectors with low wage, unskilled, dirty and monotonous jobs that German workers were increasingly unwilling to take.[28]

The charts in figure 1.5 show how dramatically things have changed since the mid-1970s. The Germans responded to the first Oil Crisis with a ban on new foreign recruitment and efforts to encourage repatriation and return migration. Paradoxically, however, as figure 1.5(a) shows, this produced a second, more far-reaching wave of family migration and a move towards permanent settlement among the existing guestworkers. Figure 1.5(b) illustrates the changing pattern of unemployment that has accompanied this trend. Despite their lowly status, the original guestworkers were, officially at least, less prone to unemployment than Germans. By the mid-1980s, they were more than twice as likely to be unemployed, partly because they were disproportionately concentrated in industries most affected by recession and economic restructuring. Most significantly, in the context of this discussion, figure 1.5(c) shows the very sharp rise since the late 1970s in the dependence of foreigners on public assistance for survival. During

1991 around 15 per cent of the foreign population at some stage received social assistance, compared with less than 5 per cent of Germans. The figures were inflated by the growth in the numbers of asylum seekers and refugees, many of whom were denied access to the labour market. However, there is much other evidence to suggest that they reflect the emergence of 'underclass' attributes (structural and juridical rather than behavioral) among the minority population more generally.[29]

Three points of more general relevance arise from these developments. First, Germany's experience highlights the importance of recognising the interdependence of social rights with political and civil rights, if European countries are to prevent the emergence of a racialised underclass, marginalised by the welfare state as well as the economy. Germany's 'foreigners' in theory enjoy virtually identical rights to welfare state programmes as German citizens. But, in practice, these have been severely circumscribed by the lesser civil rights of foreigners and, above all, because without the right to vote, they have lacked political clout. Second, Germany illustrates a failure, by no means confined to Germany, among those in politically responsible positions to develop a viable, long-term conception of policy towards immigrants and minorities. The poisonous racial flare-ups and antagonisms that have begun to plague Germany in the 1990s appear, at least partly, to be a consequence of a 'fluctuating, nonuniform, and ultimately amorphous development of policy toward foreign nationals, devoid of any definite line'.[30] The very real problems of 'integration' have to a large extent been left to ordinary Germans to sort out, but especially those in the poorest neighbourhoods.

Third, developments in Germany illustrate how the contradictions and inconsistencies of European policies towards minorities have helped 'to erode the general normative consensus on which the welfare state is built'.[31] Recent public opinion surveys in Germany, as elsewhere, show how many in the majority population have come to view the growth of minorities and immigrants as a source of the problems facing the welfare state. Certain welfare state benefits, and notions of benefit abuse, have become associated in the public mind with a visible and subordinate minority. At the same time, the welfare state's natural supporters, social democratic parties and trade unions, have found their constituents increasingly divided on the immigration and race issue. Moreover, as Freeman observes, they have been 'caught in a pincers' movement: attacked from the right for coddling immigrants, they are also criticised from within their own ranks for being insufficiently stout in defence of immigrant rights'.[32]

Social and political isolation of the poor

As the discussion has indicated, what most characterises the 'new poverty' is that it affects more acutely than in the recent past the life chances or opportunity structures of the poor. It has involved qualitative changes in the status, social relations and expectations of the poor and not just new forms of material inequality and deprivation. Terms like 'feminisation' and 'racialisation' of poverty and various explanations of poverty that now centre around labour market processes are used to convey and demonstrate these changes. However, they are evident in other ways. Compared with the 1960s, the new poor are now exposed to more grudging, bureaucratic forms of welfare that many would regard as denying them the dignity and status essential to their social citizenship. [33]

In the tougher environment on both sides of the Atlantic, the 'moral worth' of the poor (i.e. their willingness to work, sexual arrangements and honesty) is subjected to more detailed scrutiny in means-tested programmes. Recent empirical research in the United Kingdom has shown how changes in the official orientation to welfare tend to strengthen claimants' inclinations to view the state as adversary and to reduce the likelihood of their co-operation with the authorities. Rather than promoting a 'dependency culture', in the sense propounded by conservative theorists, the research pointed to more captive and disciplinary relationships among claimants:

> Caught between the administrative power of the state, the weight of adverse popular opinion and their own struggle for individual identity, many actually expressed a sense of powerlessness or of sometimes quite profound unhappiness. The disciplinary nature of the claiming experience was illustrated . . . by the way some claimants blamed themselves for their uneasy predicament. Others, however, were able to articulate ways in which they blamed the system for their powerlessness and/or unhappiness. They spoke in terms evocative of the relationship between captive and captor.[34]

It should come as no surprise that the reaction of many poor people to such trends has been a willingness to 'fiddle' the system to some degree and, among some, to revert to an alternative social economy based on illicit or semi-legal activities and earnings.

In other ways, the social and political isolation of the poor have become more marked in the 1980s and 1990s. In the United States, 'poverty ... has become more urban, more concentrated, and more firmly implanted in inner-city neighbourhoods in large metropolises, particularly in older industrial cities with immense and highly segregated black and Hispanic residents'.[35] The breakdown of social institutions in many of America's ghettos derives in part from macro-structural changes in the broader society, most notably from the declining labour market opportunities for the poor. However, central also is the way ghetto neighbourhoods have been deprived of resources, as non-poor families have moved out. They include key structural resources such as access to job-information networks and cultural resources such as conventional role models for neighbourhood children. As Wilson's work stresses:

> a social context that includes poor schools, inadequate job information networks, and a lack of legitimate employment opportunities not only gives rise to weak labour-force attachment, but increases the probability that individuals will be constrained to seek income derived from illegal or deviant activities. This weakens their attachment to the legitimate labour market even further.[36]

No European city has experienced the level of concentrated poverty and racial and ethnic segregation typical of American metropolises. Trends across the Atlantic clearly differ here, partly because of significant differences in the social and political organisation of American and European cities.[37] Nevertheless, there are many inner-city communities and outer-city public housing estates in Europe that have become progressively cut off from mainstream labour market institutions and informal job networks, creating a vicious circle of 'weak labour force attachment', growing social exclusion and rising tensions. As in the United States, evidence is now accumulating that once this process gets under way it has serious consequences for the socialisation of the next generation.[38]

Although these European communities are more mixed than in the USA, their population is invariably drawn disproportionately from various ethnic minorities. Moreover, European research has been documenting how, as it becomes more concentrated, poverty multiplies forms of deprivation, and leads to qualitative and not just material deterioration of conditions. A study in *Poverty and Labour in London*, conducted in the 1980s, notes the growing inequalities between boroughs in social and health conditions, particularly in the 'geography of death'. It also found:

> a lot more evidence of hostile and fearful relationships within local communities than did a corresponding team 17 years ago. The volume of concern about safety on the streets, burglaries and muggings has gained a major grip and affects ordinary people deeply in an increasing number of communities. . . . This makes poverty worse because it isolates people and stultifies community support and the readiness of others to offer . . . services to mitigate or compensate for the privations which old people and unemployed people experience.[39]

A weakening of community support for the poor – or what Alan Ryan has called 'the retreat from caring' – is another of the broader themes associated with the new configurations of poverty. Ryan used the phrase in a commentary on the new 'tough love' policies advocated by both sides in the 1992 US Presidential campaign, but particularly on the way even Democrats appeared to despair of the poor. Their party platform took a line that ten years earlier would have been denounced as 'blaming the victim'. Why this exasperated mood seemed so widespread was, to Ryan, a puzzle, given the low cost of the social programmes that evoked most hostility. However, he attributed it partly to despair at the apparent intractability of poverty and, more specifically, to the decline of basic formal and informal institutions in ghetto neighbourhoods. This placed severe constraints on welfare services in locating their clients but, more importantly, made it 'harder to recruit community organisers who provide grassroots support to go with government assistance'.[40]

The problem of who now speaks for the poor is a major feature of the 'new poverty' in Europe. It is partly a consequence of the dramatic erosion of trade union rights and influence. As Standing argues, unions have sometimes been castigated for representing mainly relatively secure male employees.[41] But, in reality, union membership has often in the past made a substantial difference for the most vulnerable groups in the labour market. As *Der Spiegel* showed in an investigation of racism among German youth, it is not only traditional working-class organisations that have with-drawn from some of the more detached and dislocated neighbour-hoods, but even social workers. 'It is now only the police', claimed the article, 'who speak to the skinheads'.[42]

Conclusion

This chapter has sought primarily to describe the broad challenges underlying the 'new poverty' and has avoided discussion of its more specific implications for social policy. As was emphasised at the beginning, the growth of 'new poverty' is in part a product of efforts to roll back the frontiers of the state. But, much more importantly, it reflects profound economic and social changes that challenge many of the grounding assumptions on which welfare states have been built in the past, as well as conventional divisions between different sectors of public policy. The welfare state that emerged in the first sixty years of the twentieth century was closely – and many would now argue, too inflexibly – identified with notions of collective solidarity associated with organised wage labour and class-based labour movements, and revolving primarily around the risks facing the male breadwinner. In Europe, too, fundamental to the welfare state were conceptions of citizenship that assumed a fair degree of cultural homogeneity, or at least played down the significance of historic cleavages between Cath-olics and Protestants or between various ethnic groups.

By contrast, as the twentieth century draws to a close, issues of race, ethnicity and cultural diversity loom large in all dis-cussions of citizenship. The future of the European welfare states depends crucially on the ability of European countries to widen their definitions of citizenship to embrace their new minority and immigrant communities. However – to state the obvious – this itself depends on the capacity and willingness of governments to revitalise 'social citizenship' by combating the broader marginalis-ing tendencies in the economy and welfare state that have accompanied the return of mass unemployment and the growing fragmentation of labour markets.

2 THE NEED FOR A NEW INTERNATIONAL POVERTY LINE

Peter Townsend

For hundreds of years suppositions both about the meaning of poverty and the poor have governed attempts to establish scientific methodology for the study of these phenomena. Governments and international agencies have not been exactly eager to finance genuinely independent and necessarily complex scientific work. As a consequence the vast literature on the subject is permeated with inconsistencies and contradictions. The science of poverty measurement is probably at the stage of pre-Newtonian physics.

Should the poverty line be arbitrary or objective?

I take it as axiomatic that if poverty is a measurable or observable phenomenon then the specification of a poverty 'line' to enable the poor to be distinguished from the non-poor is not an arbitrary matter. There may of course be disagreements about the criteria according to which that line should be drawn. Indeed, the set of criteria which eventually finds favour with the bulk of the scientific community may be displaced in the future by successively more sophisticated and comprehensive measures. It is not enough to examine the spread of incomes and other resources (such as wealth, property, employee welfare in kind and free or subsidised state and local services) in a population and devise an arbitrary cut-off point at a low level of income. Even small variations can have significant implications for any conclusions which may be drawn in analysis. Thus, a poverty line drawn arbitrarily at 40 per cent instead of 50 per cent of mean household expenditure lowered the poverty rate for the UK more than it did for the average EC member.[1] So we have to accept that an 'arbitrary' line for one country may not be equally arbitrary for others.

It follows that rationalisation of the choice cannot, in principle, be escaped. As the authors of a detailed comparison of two Member States of the EC concluded,

> different choices (in the construction of a measure) can change the conclusions drawn as to the relative extent of poverty in the two countries. Apparently innocuous differences in definitions can have major consequences. The degree of poverty in two countries such as France and the United Kingdom can be made to appear quite different depending on the choice of central tendency, on whether we count in terms of households or individuals, on the equivalence scale, and on the treatment of housing costs and housing benefit.[2]

Perhaps the choice of equivalence scale deserves particular attention in this catalogue of measurement ineptitude. The arbitrary choice of a poverty line has to be adjusted for different types and sizes of households. And it is logically absurd to apply criteria for any adjustment between large and small families while denying the need for criteria to draw the line in the first place. Drawing the line for each major type of household is in fact an integral part of the scientific exercise.

A third problem is in deciding what the level should be for different individuals or different income 'units' within the household. And since the demographic structure of households and society, the level of Gross National Product and its distribution, and the relationship between the levels of resources and levels of need (in *any* of the alternative scientific senses in which that term can be accepted) are continually changing, there is the fundamental problem of devising a measure which can be adjusted, or which automatically adjusts, in relation to these changes. Why should anyone take seriously the results of applying an arbitrary poverty line? Cannot governments dismiss the seriousness of any problem, and the methodology of its measurement, as so much conjecture? Drawing a line arbitrarily is like leaning forward blindfolded to pin a tail on a drawing of the backside of a donkey.

Should the poverty line be absolute or relative?

Since 1945 the international agencies have tended to prefer 'absolute' poverty as a conceptual basis for measuring poverty when comparing conditions in different countries. Or, more accurately, they have preferred this concept as a measure to be applied to the poorer 'developing' countries. The term appears to have been adopted for two reasons. One was that it seemed to refer only to the basic necessities of life – especially the minimum nutrients for ordinary physical activity. The other was that the basic necessities of life were supposed not to vary with time or place: they were fixed. However, although these reasons at first seemed acceptable to public opinion, and easy to understand, they have not stood the test of time. As societies have rapidly developed in the last 50 years and living standards have diverged and become more complex both reasons have been acknowledged to beg awkward questions. How are the necessities of life to be defined? Necessities to do what? Survive until tomorrow? Do a job of work? Provide food, fuel, shelter and clothing for a growing family? Fulfil the social obligations of marriage, family, friendship, employment, community, citizenship?

Another set of questions applies to the 'fixity' in relation to time and place. Does the same list of operational necessities apply as appropriately to a 'modern' as to a 'traditional' society, or to a 'post-industrial' as to an 'industrial' society? The question is as relevant to single countries at different intervals of time as to two or more countries at widely different stages of development. Why should a basket of marketable necessities selected, say in 1950, apply equally well in 1995 in the same country? And if that basket of goods does not need to be changed after 40 or 50 years, does not that imply that it was equally relevant to the conditions of 50 years, or 150 years previously? *And* is equally relevant to the conditions of less-developed countries like India and China in 1995?

It is only when the full potential range of comparative analysis, through time as well as location, is explored that the implications of using price indices to maintain a 'real' poverty line for different years can be properly revealed. I will give two examples. In 1991 the World Bank defined a poverty line for poor countries as $1 a day per person at 1985 prices. Is that really as applicable in 1995 as in 1985? Have not the trading and social upheavals of the late 1980s and early 1990s – internationalisation of the market, reduction of public sector subsidies and services, privatisation and the reduction of labour's share of national income – established at least the possibility of reconsidering the definition, and weighting, of basic necessities in at least a large number of those countries in 1995?

The same questions apply even more forcefully to the US poverty line. This is based on a low cost food plan derived from data from the 1955 Household Food Consumption Survey. Small changes have been made in methodology in the three decades since the measure was introduced but in 1995 the poverty line is still defined in roughly the same way. One objection is that necessities are defined more in terms of consumables than, for example, activities and services. No major investigation appears to have been made of the scope and proportion of legitimate necessities. Nor has the rationale for the selection of the minimum quantity of those necessities been adequately reviewed. Another objection is that US society has changed radically since the 1960s and it is hard to justify the continued use of an out-dated measure. And the third objection must be that since the 1960s there has been a greater disposition on the part of scientists and other professional observers to admit that individuals' membership of society and their sets of relationships and obligations within that society play a big part in the specification of individual needs.

Does the poverty line recommended for the Third World provide the right international model?

One of the continuing problems of the concern about the phenomenon of poverty is that many commentators do not seem to appreciate that the assumptions they often make about one country or region happen to be inconsistent with those they make about another country or region. Although many of them accept this readily enough when comparing, for example, the UK and India, and are a bit shame-faced if they consider they have been shown to be unconsciously racist in choosing radically different standards, they are less apologetic when asked to explain why different standards are not adopted for Scotland, Wales and Ireland than for

England. These regions are felt to be located in a common economy and social order. But what is at stake is the application of a common set of scientific principles and what these look like in operational terms.

To assist the pursuit of this objective the argument has to be examined in relation to a range of other countries. A common mistake is to define poverty differently for Eastern and Western Europe, North and South America, and First and Third Worlds. An illustration is provided by the World Bank. The Bank has conceded the 'loss of momentum during the 1980s' in reducing poverty and is developing a new strategy.[4] 'Poverty reduction is the benchmark against which our performance as a development institution must be judged', stated Lewis T. Preston, the President of the World Bank, on 28 April 1993.

But what is this benchmark? The 'poverty line' is defined at 1985 prices as '$31 per person per month, or $1 dollar per day at US purchasing power parity (PPP)'.[5] For 1990 this produces an estimate of 1,133 millions of poor in the developing world. 'An extra $0.70 per day added to the poverty line implies a doubling of the number of people counted as being poor.'[6] This revealing statistic shows how important it is to get the measure right in the first place. A previous report had 'argued the case for basing international comparisons' on this line.[7] However, this measure differs from previous measures put forward by the Bank, and is inconsistent with definitions of 'absolute poverty' and the 'poverty line' given in the same report. Thus absolute poverty is 'the position of an individual or household in relation to a poverty line the real value of which is fixed over time'; and the poverty line is 'the standard of living (usually measured in terms of income or consumption) below which people are deemed to be poor'.[8]

When these various statements are put together it is clear that the standard below which people are deemed to be poor is in practice taken to be a fixed standard, for which there is no country or regional variation and for which no criteria independent of '$1 per day' are given. For Latin America and the Caribbean the World Bank actually adopted a different poverty line of $2 per day.[9] In its 1990 report the Bank gave an impression that its conceptualisation of poverty could be extended to the industrial countries. Poverty is defined as 'the inability to attain a minimal standard of living'.[10] What exactly is this standard of living? 'Household incomes and expenditures per capita are adequate yardsticks.'[11]

However, there are drawbacks because income and expenditure measures do not capture dimensions of welfare like access to public goods and services, clean drinking water and other 'common property' resources.

This admission does not prompt scientific enquiry to produce a more consistent or 'objective' poverty line. The argument proceeds in a ramshackle way. All that appears to be necessary is to examine the drawbacks in relation to 'some norm' – namely a 'consumption-based' poverty line.[12] This 'can be thought of' as comprising two elements: the expenditure necessary to buy a minimum standard of nutrition and other basic necessities; and a further amount that varies from country to country, reflecting the cost of participating in the everyday life of society'.[13] The first is believed to be unproblematic. The cost of caloric intakes and other necessities can be calculated by 'looking at the prices of the foods that make up the diets of the poor'. The second 'is far more subjective; in some countries indoor plumbing is a luxury, but in others it is a "necessity" '.[14] This is a very odd statement. In what sense is the need for indoor plumbing, as distinct from the need for food, 'subjective'? And when is it a 'luxury' and when a 'necessity'? Does not the cost of food, as much as the cost of plumbing, reflect participation in the everyday life of society? If the latter is a 'luxury' in some societies does that mean that food never is?

In this account of the World Bank's procedures I have tried to concentrate on the unexplained and unresearched elements in the specification. Indeed, at one point the text suggests that country-specific poverty lines are plotted against per capita consumption for 'thirty four developing and industrial countries', but the figure on the same page shows only the plotted figures for the poorest 12 countries among them. For the 22 richer countries country-specific poverty lines are not plotted. The Bank's poverty measurement cannot, therefore, remain acceptable in international practice.

Other international agencies compound the problem. The poverty line is defined by UNDP as 'that income level below which a minimum nutritionally adequate diet plus essential non-food requirements are not affordable'.[15] The steps by which a minimum nutritionally adequate diet, and 'essential non-food requirements' can be defined as appropriate for different countries, and the criteria according to which these can be said to be 'affordable' are not investigated.

A report for the International Fund for Agricultural Development comes close to this perspective but seems to introduce a measure of flexibility into a 'fixed' poverty line by taking note of measures which originate nationally and which depend on more sophisticated investigation of changes in consumption as well as consumption prices. Thus the poverty line is 'a commodity bundle tied to the minimum requirement (calories and protein for food, and some notional minimum for non-food items), and the determination of an appropriate set of prices to be applied to individual commodities to calculate the poverty expenditure and income'.[16]

The ILO has contributed over the years to a more 'structural' interpretation of poverty and its causes.[17] In particular, its work on the structure of the labour market and questions of access to that market help to balance the monetarist perspectives of IMF and World Bank. The ILO began in the 1970s to show the part to be played in explaining poverty by lack of community utilities or infrastructure – water, sanitation, health centres, primary schools, and transport. The development of measures of collective or community need, as distinct from individual need, as a contribution to understanding poverty and its alleviation, deserves renewed attention. Thus, some commentators have pointed out that the World Bank's 1990 report on poverty

> represents a step away from neoliberalism and back toward the Bank's attitude of the 1960s: that the continuing existence of the poor in poor nations is the development problem. Indeed, the insistence (in the Bank's annual development reports) on remedying water and air pollution resembles nothing more strongly than 20–year-old strategies aimed at satisfying developing countries' basic needs.[18]

The ILO preoccupations of the 1970s are back in fashion.[19]

Do the poverty lines in the rich countries set the right example?

Any reference to the rich countries illustrates the nature of the scientific problem. The United States, for example, accepts a poverty line based on assumptions far removed from those applied to the poorer countries. The line is based on the least costly budget demonstrated to achieve adequate nutrition and conform in its overall distribution with the budgets of low-income families in the

US – the specific amounts varying according to household size and composition, and being adjusted each year in accordance with price changes. In 1990 the poverty line varied from $6,652 for a person living alone to $26,848 for a household of nine or more members.[20] Depending on size and type of household, therefore, the poverty line in the US varied in 1990 from over $6,000 to $3,000 per person per annum (or between 18 and 8 dollars a day).

This means that at *comparable purchasing standards* the US poor are allowed between eight and 18 times as much income as in countries like China, India and Mozambique to attract that designation.

The scientific implication may not be that the US poverty line must be lowered. Available evidence suggests, on the contrary, that Third World poverty lines should be raised substantially. Everything turns on the scope and generosity of the criteria used to define the poverty line, as well as the readiness to apply the same criteria to countries at widely different stages of national economic affluence.

Different criteria from those in the US apply in Europe. In launching the Second European Poverty Programme (1985–89) the Council of Ministers defined the poor as 'persons whose resources (material, cultural and social) are so limited as to exclude them from the minimum acceptable way of life in the Member State in which they live'.[21] This definition was reiterated subsequently in a report from the Statistical Office of the European Communities.[22] The concept of 'resources' included in this definition had been defined in a previous Council decision as 'goods, cash income, plus services from public and private resources'.[23]

Sadly, criteria for giving effect to this definition were never worked out in the formulation of successive anti-poverty programmes, from the first programme of 1975–79 onwards. Instead, the number of those with less than 50 per cent, and later 40 per cent, of average disposable income per person in each member country was regarded as 'a good indicator of the extent of poverty'.[24] The reasons for the adjective 'good' were not specified. This indicator is in practice a 'relative income standard' – a term used to differentiate the standard, which is based on the choice of a point in the spread of income, from one which is based on criteria external to income.[25]

The problem has been compounded in reports from sub-divisions of the EC and in reports from other agencies (for example,

Eurostat, 1990, which differed in approach primarily by taking expenditure rather than income as the governing criterion in selecting 40 per cent and 50 per cent of the mean).

In 1990 this standard would have provided a poverty line for a person living alone of approximately 3,500, or, at US exchange rates, nearly $6,000. For a family of four the poverty line would have been about $17,000 per annum, compared with a figure of $13,359 for the US poverty line for the same family. Thus, although the US and Europe follow different procedures in measurement, in practice they both apply assumptions in constructing a poverty line radically more generous than those applied by international agencies to poor countries.

I doubt whether this form of discrimination can be allowed to persist. Our conventional methods of discriminating between the needs of (predominantly black) Third World countries and the needs of (predominantly white) First World countries smack of conscious, or at least unconscious, racism. Once the poverty line is defined in a discriminatory fashion there is a knock-on effect. The collected evidence becomes skewed. Theories are evolved to explain distorted evidence; and policies are correspondingly evolved to suit that distorted evidence – but not reality. This happens because international agencies and others dodge the responsibility of defining the precise scope of human and social needs, and because they do not specify criteria for estimating the collective and individual costs of meeting those needs *minimally*.

A definition is therefore required which stands the test of time and is genuinely international. The problem tends to have been glossed over in reports on the poorer countries by the international agencies. Thus, the arbitrary selection of $1 per day as a poverty line conforms with an ideology which pre-supposes that economic growth is the principal strategy to overcome poverty.[26] It also conforms with an ideology which suggests that the needs of poor countries are less than those of the rich countries. This carries imputations which cannot be accepted in the 1990s. It also results in entirely misplaced strategies.

Defining a poverty line across countries and within countries for different years

There is a close link between the task of specifying a common definition of poverty across countries and specifying a definition which will be appropriate for each country at different times. Societies will tend to change in crucial respects in successive decades – in terms of wealth, type of employment and forms of social and cultural institutions. But there will be continuities as well as discontinuities. At successive stages of the history of different societies, social scientists have defined a poverty line for those societies which represents something very different from applying a price index to adjust for inflation and reconstitute the *same* poverty line in *real* terms. Scholars have called attention, for example, to the income elasticity of the poverty line.[27]

There is evidence for different countries that minimum budgets devised by experts and low income measures based on public opinion tend to rise more closely in accordance with trends in GDP than in conformity only with price increases. For example, 'there is an impressive body of evidence that in the United States, both 'expert'-devised poverty/subsistence budgets and 'subjective' low-income measures rise in real terms when the real income of the population rises'.[28] The evidence which is cited is impressive and includes answers to a routine Gallup Poll question, budget studies in New York city between 1903 and 1959, and a set of minimum subsistence budgets traced between 1905 and 1960.

Thus, a Gallup Poll question 'what is the smallest amount of money a family of four (husband, wife and two children) needs each week to get along in this community?' has been posed regularly in surveys over many years. Fisher cites a series of review studies from the 1960s onwards. They show, for spans of ten or more years, that the average amount specified by respondents rises between 0.6 per cent and 0.85 per cent for every 1.0 per cent rise in the real average income of the population.[29] The standards set by household budget experts have tended to follow the same pattern.

Can an international poverty line be developed?

In principle there is a solution to the question raised in this chapter. It is to identify forms of deprivation and multiple deprivation in relation to the whole range of material conditions and social activities and customs in all countries, and to investigate what thresholds of income (and other resources for both individuals and community) can be shown to eliminate or greatly reduce such deprivation. That is a complex scientific assignment, but the interrelationship of forms of nutritional, material, environmental, work-related and social deprivation is no more complex than the interrelationship of genes or physical nuclei or atoms. Once a scientific problem is comprehensively specified, means can be found to illuminate and then to resolve it.

One final step is necessary to prepare the ground for the construction of an international 'poverty line'. It is to call attention to the overwhelming evidence of the rapid internationalisation of economic and social conditions. The international market is becoming the central global institution. Multinational corporations and international agencies have assumed much larger powers in determining events in many countries. Groups of nation-states, like the EC, are increasingly acting in a concerted way to facilitate international finance and commerce. The power of the nation-state is logically waning as a consequence. National boundaries are becoming less important, though one outcome of the regionalisation of some nation-states has been the expression of petty nationalism and ethnic rivalries. The costs of labour in the rich countries are being driven towards a convergence with labour costs in the poor countries.

Despite annual and country variations, the level of overall unemployment in the rich countries has steadily increased since the 1960s. Among the rich countries the US and the UK are not alone in experiencing widening inequality, and growing poverty, in the 1980s and 1990s. Already there is evidence of international drug networks wreaking havoc in the inner cities of Latin America and North America alike, and havoc too in the inner cities of Europe. Public facilities and services are declining everywhere, especially in countries turning over to market privatisation. Public housing moulders. Protective labour and health and safety associations are undermined and no longer exercise a balancing influence. Small wonder that there is mounting evidence of Third World conditions and wages in First World countries. There are even respects in which ghetto conditions in some parts of the richest countries of the world are worse than the conditions of most of the rural poor in Third World countries.

In 2050 the inequalities of rich and poor in each nation may reach levels which are more striking than *average* differences today between rich and poor countries. This is illustrated in Figures 2.1 and 2.2. Figure 2.1 shows the two forms of inequality – the huge difference between rich and poor countries when income is standardised in relation to the *average* income per person in the United States; and the already huge inequality in most countries between the average income of the richest 20 per cent and that of the poorest 20 per cent.

Figure 2.2 shows groups of countries categorised according to their income, again expressed as a percentage per person of the corresponding income per person in the US. The figure shows that while there are sharp differences between the poorest countries and the richest countries, the *poorest* 20 per cent in the 22 high income countries have an average income only about the same as the *average* of that in the 43 'lower middle income' countries, and only about twice that of the richest 20 per cent in the 40 'low income' countries. The problems of poverty, and of current impoverishment, are evidently more widespread than generally assumed or, indeed, documented.

Statistics giving the average income and the distribution of income in each country, imply that the total national income, and its distribution, are the responsibility of that country. But just as the statistics for each country have to be adjusted to represent 'real' variations in relation to an international measure of income, so they have to be qualified in relation both to the local conditions to which that 'income' applies, and the causes of the level and distribution of that income. More specifically, some of the important causes of unemployment, homelessness, low wages, poor health, weakened public services, lost employment rights and reduced social security benefits, are to be found outside the sovereignty of both rich and poor states in which they can be identified. Like plagues, economic and political ideologies can be contagious.

While this account of trends is expressed here in very general terms, and is of course subject to detailed qualification and amendment, that account shows the importance of adopting scientific

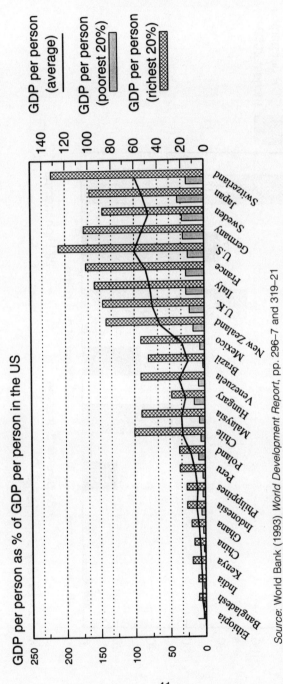

Source: World Bank (1993) *World Development Report*, pp. 296–7 and 319–21
Note: GDP per Person for 1991 US=100

Figure 2.1   The Poor and the Rich of Different Countries According to their Income Standardised in 'International Purchasing' Dollars

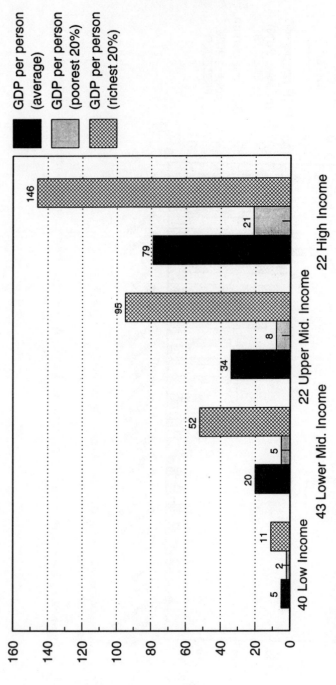

Figure 2.2 GDP Per Person as a Percentage of GDP Per Person in the US

Note: GDP per person for 1991, US=100

measures and indicators which properly capture those trends, so that they can be explained and acted upon.

What are the alternative poverty lines for the UK?

I believe the argument for an international poverty line sets the scene for the discussion of what might be an appropriate adaptation, if only an interim adaptation, for rich countries like the UK and the US, as well as for the poorest countries of the world. The poverty line in the US, and in countries like India and Ethiopia, will be the subject of separate papers, which I am preparing.[30] As an example I propose here to review alternative standards which might be adapted for use in the UK. There are a number of interesting variations on offer.

The World Bank's 'global' standard

This is a 'universal poverty line [which] is needed to permit cross-country comparison and aggregation'.[31] Poverty is defined as 'the inability to attain a minimal standard of living'.[32] Despite its acknowledgement of the difficulties in capturing the contribution to standards of living of public goods and common-property resources in any measure of poverty the World Bank settles for a standard which is 'consumption-based' – and which, as discussed above, comprises 'two elements; the expenditure necessary to buy a minimum standard of nutrition and other basic necessities and a further amount that varies from country to country, reflecting the cost of participating in the everyday life of society'.[33] The first of these was stated to be 'relatively straightforward' because it could be calculated by 'looking at the prices of the foods that make up the diets of the poor'.[34] However, the second was 'far more subjective'; in some countries indoor plumbing is a luxury; but in others it is a 'necessity'.[35] For operational purposes the second was set aside and the former was assessed as PPP (Purchasing Power Parity) $370 per year per person at 1985 prices for all the poorest developing countries.

Strengths

The standard is simple to comprehend and apply. It does not depend on the arduous and continuous collection and compilation of data about types as well as amounts of resources, changing patterns of necessities and changing construction of standards of living.

Weaknesses

It is not in fact a 'global' poverty line at all. It is not assumed to be applicable to countries other than the poorest. On the Bank's own admission an international poverty line which is more than 'consumption-based' should, ideally, be constructed. No cost is in fact estimated for the second 'participatory' element of the definition. So the logic of the Bank's own argument is not followed: therefore the minimum value of the poverty line is underestimated and the number of poor in the world also underestimated.

The first element of the definition of the poverty line is neither rigorously investigated nor defended. I mean that the type, number and amounts of necessities *other* than food are ignored. Equally important, variations in the sheer quantity of the diet required among populations with widely varying work and other activity obligations and customs, as well as in the types of diet socially preferred or indeed available in local markets, and at what cost, are left unexplored. Again, the possibility that the second element of the definition might apply to the poorest countries, and therefore demand scientific investigation and expert discussion, is also ignored. And although the Bank constructed a graph which was supposed to show the rising real per capita value of 'country-specific' poverty lines in relation to average per capita consumption, the graph did not in fact fulfil this intention; it merely showed an upper and a lower poverty line fixed by the Bank in dollars at 1985 prices for a small number of poor countries in relation to the average per capita consumption in those countries. The procedure offers no basis for UK adaptation.

European relative income standard

This is a standard which depends only on a criterion of low income rather than any independent condition or state of need. The choice of the standard seems to depend just on consideration of the distribution of income, and political as well as social values are plainly embodied in the choice. The most common indicator is 40 per cent, or 50 per cent, of the mean disposable household income, or expenditure, in a country. I have proposed the epithet 'European' mainly because from the 1970s European agencies and research institutes took the lead in using income cut-off points as a means of identifying the numbers and composition of the poor, in contrast to the different approaches to poverty line construction in both the United States and, for the Third World, the World Bank and other international agencies.

In one UK study started at the end of the 1960s this standard of poverty was distinguished from the state's standard and from the deprivation standard.[36] However, the UK's membership of the EC is leading to the absorption of national income measures into more conventional EC practice.

A variation on the relative income standard described above is the identification of income strata, such as decile groups or quintile groups, below average household income. This is the standard represented by the Households Below Average Income analyses carried out every two years (in 1994 it became annual) in the United Kingdom.[37] Other 'low-income' measure have been reviewed extensively in Canadian work.[38]

Strengths

Most European states conduct income and expenditure surveys, and maintain administrative information about income distribution, mainly for tax purposes. These data are easily available for analysis, and can be subjected to some degree of standardisation for purposes of comparison. The results may vary from year to year, proportionate to population, and are therefore of more significance in relation to rates of economic growth, unemployment and employment, and demographic change, than fixed divisions by decile or quintile group.

Weaknesses

The selection of a cut-off point low on the income scale is not related to any strict criteria of need or deprivation. The selection of cut-off point does in practice hold important implications for each country, which are only now beginning to be analysed and reported.[39] Different choices in the construction, and operational application, of the cut-off points can lead to surprisingly diverse results in the extent and composition of 'poverty' in different countries. The variation of the European relative income standard used by the UK (the Households Below Average Income series) lacks the advantages, and shares the disadvantages, of the European standard. It also has a number of additional weaknesses – for example in the choice of median and not also mean in analysing information for each of the lower deciles; in obscuring year to year trends; and in making very difficult comparisons between certain substantial sub-categories of poor.[40]

The state's standard of poverty

The minimum standards of benefit (or wage) sanctioned and institutionalised by the state, usually on test of means, have been treated in many studies as a 'social' standard of poverty. In some countries these are called social or national assistance, or income support, scales and in France the RMI (Revenu Minimum d'Insertion). Thus, by comparing household and individual income and expenditure derived from surveys with the minimum entitlements for comparable households and individuals, estimates can be produced of the numbers in the population with incomes of less than, the same as, or slightly above, these specific levels. This approach was pioneered in the 1960s and adopted for many different countries.[41]

Strengths

Governments are obliged to concede that the standard of low income exists (because it is one which they have established through legislation and administrative follow up) and can be debated in terms of its 'adequacy'. While they may argue that families are sometimes expected to have small amounts of resources additional to benefit they are nonetheless under pressure to rationalise the minimum levels of benefit, and in that process offer indirect if not direct criteria of the contribution the levels of benefit are supposed to make to the reduction of poverty.

Weaknesses

The standard institutionalised by the state may have little relationship to any scientific, or even social, criteria of need or deprivation. Moreover, there are difficulties in using the standard either to describe historical trends, or to make comparisons between countries. Periods when the levels of benefit have been relatively generous, and countries where the levels are relatively generous, produce disproportionately high rates of poverty, as the DSS in the UK has been quick to point out.

Household budget standards

These depend on surveys of consumption. One influential example in the UK was produced following a series of research studies sponsored by the Joseph Rowntree Foundation.[42] There are two standards, a *low-cost budget*, and a *modest-but-adequate* budget. The low-cost budget 'includes items which more than two-thirds of the population regard as "necessities" or which more than three quarters of the population actually have. Only the cheapest items are included. It therefore represents a frugal level of living'.[43] Authority for the detailed specifications was derived from 'nutritionists, home economists and social scientists specialising in the domestic economy', and from a range of similar work completed in the United States (from 1946), Sweden, the Netherlands, Norway, and Germany.[44] This approach is intended to go beyond meagre definitions of either minimum subsistence or absolute poverty.[45] It draws on a range of previous work in the UK, including that on the 'cost' of children.[46]

The methodology corresponds with precedents set in a large number of countries. For example, in a review of alternative budget-based expenditure norms prepared for a panel on poverty measurement of the Committee on National Statistics of the US National Academy, Watts distinguishes between three alternative budget standards: 'market basket', 'gross-up' and 'category' standards. The first covers necessities picked out from a wide range of consumer purchases. The second concentrates on minimum food costs, and 'grosses up' the total budget from estimates of those costs. This approach in fact closely resembles the procedure followed over the years in the construction of the US poverty line, following Orshansky's recommendations.[47] The third establishes a small number (usually 7–10) of spending categories – such as spending on food, housing, transport, health care, child and other dependent care, clothing and clothing maintenance, and personal, e.g. dental care and haircuts. Watts concludes that the third offers the 'most promising of the budget-based approaches'.[48]

Strengths

The strength of the methodology lies in its apparent practicality – using expenditure data and professional expertise about low-cost budgeting. This brings expert pressure to bear on government policies. As the report concludes: 'If the low-cost budget costs 36 per week more than the Income Support scales, then government can be asked to specify which budget items they believe that claimants should do without'.[49] The approach is also realistic – being dependent on country-specific information, which requires a lot of effort to collect and keep up-to-date.[50] And the fact that the standard is practical and specific makes it publicly and politically plausible.

Weaknesses

Among the problems of this methodology is the circularity of the reasoning. The transformation of actual amounts and patterns of household expenditure into *desirable* or *necessary* amounts and patterns of expenditure must turn on criteria which are scientifically independent of expenditure. Otherwise the reasoning is tautological. It is important to investigate empirically *needs* independent of budgetary resources and outlay. It is not the intensive scrutiny and elaborate analysis of household expenditure which will provide the answer to what level of income is required by different households to manage on, and satisfy their everyday material and social needs, in present day society. It is the investigation, across the whole of society, of activity conditions, customs, patterns and role obligations, on the part of interacting groups and communities as well as individuals and households – to find whether there is a high correlation between level of activity or deprivation and level of income. The social and material correlates or effects of low level of income or expenditure have to be investigated – not the composition or scope and balance of that income or expenditure.

The desirability of making reference to external criteria applies as much to the choice of equivalence scales as to the selected level on the income scale. The income *needed* by different members of a household in relation to its (usually male) head cannot be derived from the existing amount and division between them of expenditure or income. The elucidation of the latter will determine the former. Forms of discrimination which exist in contemporary society, to do with gender, ethnicity, disability and age, for example, are implicit in the current or conventional disposition of either income or expenditure. Unless these forms of discrimination can be corrected by means of the application to the divisions of income and expenditure of independent criteria of need they will be passed across and embodied as assumptions in the formulation of the 'household budget standards'.

The methodology is also weighted too heavily towards the resources required to buy market commodities, rather than the resources required to satisfy *collective* needs for services and utilities, and to fulfil *social obligations* – in parenthood, work-roles and citizenship, for example. In other words, the respects in which the need is collective, and in which resources therefore have to be collective too, is not investigated.

Perceived deprivation

One alternative to budget standards is to find the level of income below which perceived deprivation multiplies. One pioneering study presented a random sample of the national population with a long list of commodities, customs and activities to find which and how many of them were perceived as 'necessary' and also as 'affordable'.[51] The results of the survey were that more than 7 million of the population, or 14 per cent, were in poverty in the sense that they could not afford three or more of the necessities of life, as defined by a majority of the sample. The 1990 updating of this approach is now available.[52]

Strengths

The perception in a population of what is necessary and affordable provides an independent criterion in the construction of a poverty line. Rather than elites, and collections of officially approved sets of income and expenditure statistics, being in the driving seat, the opinions and attitudes of a cross-section of the population are explored. The evidence is direct and first-hand. The realistic 'context' of the approach should also be recognised. Thus, opinions are sought about the priority that should be accorded to certain major social services and public utilities, as well as popular notions of 'poverty'. Thus, compared with some other sources of evidence, considerable sections of the population refer to social injustice as a cause of poverty rather than 'laziness and lack of willpower'.

Weaknesses

The elucidation of opinion takes precedence over the elucidation of behaviour. Although this is understandable, because of the limited resources (in this instance) available for research, it does mean that there can be no easy check on the extent to which people's views about need correspond with the behaviour which may be said to be *revelatory* of need. The same point might be made about the selection of the list of needs and the number of needs applying at any particular time to households which makes them significant. Human priorities have to be ascertained in terms of observed actions and not only expressed preferences. People reveal their priorities in the way they act when short of cash as well as in expressions of their opinion. Again, the investigation of individual preferences sits more easily with pre-suppositions about individuals and households as consumers (and therefore mainstream economic theory and ideology) than it does with individuals and households as agents of social institutions and structures. This calls attention to the importance of locating definitions of major social phenomena within particular theories (for example, monetarist, neo-classical, functionalist) and particular ideologies. The definition of conditions, and the identification of causes of those conditions must lie outside the perceptions of individuals. The 'consensual judgement of society' is a necessary, but insufficient, criterion upon which to build a poverty line.

Relative deprivation

This is a standard built on the idea that in all societies there is a threshold of low income or resources marking a change in the capacity of human beings to meet the needs, material and social, enjoined by that society. Some such idea is the only one logically available to distinguish poverty from inequality – whether subjectively or objectively. In descending a scale of income (or income combined with the value of other types of resources) instances of deprivation steadily increase. But below a certain level of income the forms and instances of deprivation are hypothesised to multiply disproportionately to the fall of income. Information is collected about both material and social needs – in the sense of role obligations, customs and activities.[53]

Strengths

The investigation and analysis of the *range* as well as the *type* of human needs is in principle comprehensive. By establishing what people do and don't do at different levels of income, generalisations can be developed about the priorities of human action, relationships and consumption, and what can still be said to be 'normative' at the lowest threshold of income. If the broad assumption about the cohesion of society holds, then the identification of the level of income below which membership of that society and conformity with its customs, begins to collapse, is a proper scientific objective. In nearly all countries some such assumption, when poverty 'matters', is of course made – though attention is usually restricted to food and other material rather than also to social needs. The more comprehensive approach lends itself to cross-national and cross-cultural comparison much better than country-specific, or needs-specific approaches. It also lends itself to the elucidation of the effects of discriminatory policies so that the needs, as distinct from the institutionalised living standards of men and women, disabled and elderly people, racial minorities and other groups, may be brought to light.

Weaknesses

Scientific research is inevitably costly and time-consuming, given the deliberately comprehensive approach. This applies in particular to the selection (from that research) of indicators of deprivation, the assumptions which have to be made about the definition of the 'society' to which the operational measure of poverty applies. This qualification also applies to the degree to which the society's internal cultures and groups are sufficiently cohesive or integrated to warrant both the establishment of what is 'normative' behaviour and what balance of types of resources which can be incorporated into a common measure of resources or income.

Conclusions

The value of hunting down the extraordinary global variation in approach to the construction of poverty lines is, first, to expose the lack of scientific basis in cross-national as well as country-specific work, and in that process to show the discriminatory features of definitions which have been put into operational practice. This is a scientific and also international objective.

Second, the difficult task of arriving at an international formulation has sharp implications for each country, compelling discussion of scientific criteria of deprivations but also 'adequate' resources or income. This will mean radical change in current orthodoxies. It is bound to prompt a lot more appropriate research – not only into the deprivation and the stultification of the role obligations and role potentialities of the poor, but into the disproportionate seizure and domination of resources on the part of the rich. Most practical of all, it will afford more relevant criteria of the adequacy of minimum standards of income – as in a minimum wage or levels of social assistance, or income support.

I make the optimistic assumption too that if this (deliberately empirical and comprehensive or international) approach can make some inroads into present unsatisfactory, and indeed unsubstantiated, concepts, measures, theories and policies about poverty, there will be some chance of redressing the contemporary balance between ideology and science, and between ideology and the democratic representation of need. That will necessarily threaten the prevailing extreme (and unjustifiable) global hierarchy of power.

Therefore, the partial approaches towards an 'international' poverty line which have been made by the World Bank and other international agencies, placing undue emphasis on the idea of 'absolute' poverty, and by European agencies, placing undue emphasis on a relative income standard, cannot be sustained. Each of these approaches distorts more than it helps – when related to international social relations and conditions. Again, the country-specific household or family budget standards developed in a variety of countries, including the US, Belgium, Germany and the UK, are insufficiently addressed to international market causes of 'country-specific' income inequality and poverty. The character of their methodology is nationally introspective. They also tend to be caught in the convolutions of circularity of reasoning. Patterns of expenditure are regenerated as patterns of need for income.

'Perceived' and 'relative' deprivation therefore have brighter prospects for national and international use. They have complementary advantages as scientific instruments and as socially revelatory and practical standards for the investigation and reduction of poverty.

Appendix: glossary of principal definitions

World Bank. Absolute poverty is 'the position of an individual or household in relation to a poverty line the real value of which is fixed over time'. The poverty line is 'the standard of living (usually measured in terms of income or consumption) below which people are deemed to be poor'.[55] This is interpreted as a 'consumption-based' poverty line[56] comprising two elements: 'the expenditure necessary to buy a minimum standard of nutrition and other basic necessities; and a further amount that varies from country to country, reflecting the cost of participating in the everyday life of society'.[57]

UNDP. The poverty line is defined by UNDP as 'that income level below which a minimum nutritionally adequate diet plus essential non-food requirements are not affordable'.[58]

European relative income standard. In launching the Second European Poverty Programme (1985–89) the Council of Ministers defined the poor as 'persons whose resources (material, cultural and social) are so limited as to exclude them from the minimum acceptable way of life in the Member State in which they live'.[59]

Household budget standard. There are two standards, a *low-cost budget*, and a *modest-but-adequate* budget. The low-cost budget 'includes items which more than two-thirds of the population regard as 'necessities' or which more than three quarters of the population actually have. Only the cheapest items are included. It therefore represents a frugal level of living'.[60]

Relative deprivation. 'People are relatively deprived if they cannot obtain, at all or sufficiently, the conditions of life – that is, the diets, amenities, standards and services – which allow them to play the roles, participate in the relationships and follow the customary behaviour which is expected of them by virtue of their membership of society. If they lack or are denied resources to obtain access to these conditions of life and so fulfil membership of society they may be said to be in poverty'.[61]

3 WOMEN IN POVERTY

Ruth Lister

'Whether they are young or old, with or without men, caring for children or other dependants, women are more likely than men to be poor.'[1] This statement by Caroline Glendinning and Jane Millar, who have done much to raise awareness in the social policy community about women's poverty, relates to the UK but is of wider relevance. It is not a recent phenomenon, as sometimes implied by the idea of the feminisation of poverty, for as Jane Lewis and David Piachaud have noted 'the simple fact is that throughout the last century women have always been much poorer than men'.[2] Nevertheless, the notion of the feminisation of poverty does help to highlight the extent to which women are disadvantaged by current employment and social policies and the consequent restructuring of labour markets and welfare states.

Despite women's longstanding relative disadvantage, there appears to be little official recognition – either at national or EC level – of the gendered nature of poverty. Thus, most national and EC poverty statistics are not broken down according to sex. Nor do relevant policy discussions tend to consider the particular implications of different options for women. This is, perhaps, odd at EC level, in light of the priority given to equal opportunities between women and men. It reflects a more widespread failure to integrate equal opportunities and anti-poverty perspectives. Such an integration is necessary at every level: policy-making and execution, academic and practitioner, if women's poverty is not to remain invisible and is to be addressed.

The un-gendered understanding of poverty typical of European policy-makers contrasts with the approach increasingly taken by international agencies in Third World countries. Here it is recognised that effective anti-poverty interventions are best directed primarily towards women both as the managers of poverty and as potential agents of change.

55

The first aim of this paper is to make the case for a gendered understanding of poverty on the basis of four main points:

(i)   the simple quantitative fact that women are more likely than men to be poor;

(ii) that the structural causes of women's poverty have to be understood in relation to their position in the family as well as the labour market and in relation to the ideology of economic dependency which links the two;

(iii) that poverty is experienced by individuals and that therefore one has to look behind the statistics based on households or families at the circumstances of the individuals within families. This can reveal hidden female poverty;

(iv) that women's relationship to poverty is characterised by their taking the main responsibility for and strain of managing it and of negotiating with the institutions of the welfare state. More positively, women also often play a very active role in community-based initiatives to combat poverty.

Second, I will argue that women's poverty constitutes a challenge to reform our social security system and to the way that we approach any proposals for reform.

(Dis)counting women's poverty

As noted, women are rendered invisible in official and unofficial estimates of the incidence of poverty. For Great Britain, the Child Poverty Action Group has estimated that, in 1989, there were approximately 5.1 million women as against just under 3.4 million men living on or below the social assistance level, using official measurements based on the family as the unit.[3] From the official *Social Security Statistics* it is possible to calculate that nearly two-thirds of adults supported by the social assistance income support scheme are women.[4] Analysis of the Family Expenditure Survey reveals that women are over-represented in the lowest deciles, both on the basis of their individual income (or lack of it) and also when taking account of the incomes of other households members. In the latter case, two-thirds of adults in the poorest households are women, according to Steven Webb.[5]

I do not have similar figures for other countries or even for the EU as a whole. Nevertheless, it is fair to say that, even in countries with more progressive social policies than our own, women's economic position is, on average, inferior to men's. Certainly, Eurostat calculations show that in all the member states studied, except the Netherlands, female-headed households have higher than average poverty rates. The different incidence of poverty between male and female-headed households is especially high in the UK, Ireland, Portugal and France.[6]

Understanding women's poverty is not, however, just a question of numbers. While it is important that there is a wider awareness of the extent of women's poverty, its particular causes and nature need to be built into our understanding of poverty generally, rather than separated out, as if of relevance only to a minority. If we look at the structural causes of male poverty, they lie primarily in their position in relation to the labour market. This is true for women too, except that their labour market position is also mediated by their position in the family. Thus any analysis of the structural causes of women's poverty has to look at the relationship between their position in the family and the labour market.

Women in the family

Women's continued main responsibility for the care of children and of older or disabled adults inhibits their labour market participation. The exact nature of the impact of women's caring responsibilities varies between countries. An analysis of women's position in the labour market in the EU has suggested that the critical factor is different countries' general strategies for dealing with family obligations.[7] The analysis focuses solely on childcare, reflecting the insufficient attention still paid to the effects of other caring obligations on labour market participation. Yet UK research has exposed the poverty experienced by many carers, especially female ones, and the short and long term impact caring has on their position in the labour market.[8] At the same time, disabled women are drawing attention to the fact that they represent the majority of disabled people and that income maintenance and service policies must respect the needs of both women who provide *and* women who receive care.[9]

The analysis of the EU divides Member States into four rough groups:

(i) where children do not influence economic activity rates; Denmark is the only example;

(ii) where children have a minimal impact; France is the main example;

(iii) where difficulties in combining paid work and family responsibilities are 'resolved' through part-time work; the UK is the prime example;

(iv) where the first child results in a marked drop in economic activity; the Netherlands and Ireland are the main examples given.

Access to childcare varies widely within the EU, with Denmark, Italy, France and Belgium at one extreme, with a high proportion of pre-school children covered, and the UK, Luxembourg, the Netherlands and Ireland at the other extreme. Childcare has emerged as a key theme in EU Poverty 3 projects in the UK. In the former socialist countries of Central and Eastern Europe, childcare facilities are being cut back drastically. The presence of children is likely to start effecting labour market participation in a way that it has not done in recent years in these countries.

The implications for women's poverty of their caring responsibilities generally only receives recognition when women become solely responsible for the care of children as lone parents. Then they become a recognisable poverty category.

The EU has highlighted the growth in the number of lone-parent families as a significant factor in the overall increase in poverty in the Union and in the shift in the burden of poverty towards those of working age.[10] In a number of Member States, including Great Britain, the trend has been towards increased reliance on social assistance among lone mothers. In Great Britain for instance, between 1979 and 1992, the proportion of all lone-parent families reliant on social assistance rose from 38 per cent to 70 per cent, with lone mothers more likely to be in this position than lone fathers. Overall, the position of lone-parent families deteriorated relative to average living standards during the 1980s in Great Britain.[11] The Final Report of the Second European Poverty Programme noted that lone-parent families' financial situation, in any one country, depends largely on the proportion able to take paid work.[12] This is supported by a York University study of six EU and several other countries that found as labour market participation increased, poverty decreased. It also found that the proportion of lone mothers in poverty was, on average, twice that of lone fathers. Lone mothers are most likely to be economically active in Denmark and France and least likely in Ireland.[13]

Women in the labour market

Clearly, labour market participation is an important determinant of the economic position of lone mothers and of women generally. However, it cannot be assumed that a job of itself provides a ladder out of poverty and economic dependency.

Overall in the EU there has been an increase in female labour market participation (now being mirrored by a decrease in Eastern Europe). But women are joining a labour market which continues to be segregated, both horizontally and vertically, on gender lines and which, consequently, rewards them, on average, at lower rates of pay than men. Moreover, the increase in women's employment has been and is predicted to continue to be mainly in 'atypical' jobs, i.e. part-time and/or temporary.

A recent Equal Opportunities Commission report on the implications of the Single European Market for women concluded that it is 'no exaggeration to speak of a trend towards precariousness in female employment'.[14] It pointed, too, to a trade-off, to the detriment of women, between their quantitative and qualitative position in the workforce. Migrant women are particularly disadvantaged and over-concentrated in low paid, insecure forms of employment.

In 1987, 28 per cent of women workers in the EU worked part-time, compared with barely 4 per cent of men. Part-time work is more common in Northern than Southern Europe.[15] However, in Britain at least, part-time work is much less common among black women than among white women. This is thought to reflect the lower wages available, on average, to black male workers and also the greater prevalence of female-headed Afro-Caribbean households.

In the UK, the trend towards increased part-time working has been matched by a reduction in the average number of hours worked, with a big increase in the proportion working fewer than 16 hours a week and therefore outside full statutory employment protection. In general, part-time work is associated with shorter hours in the UK, Denmark and the Netherlands than in the EU as a whole.[16] Many women prefer part-time work as a way of combining paid work with the domestic and caring responsibilities which still rest mainly on their shoulders (see below). But they tend to pay a heavy price in terms of poor pay and working conditions and loss of employment and social rights. Women are also over-represented in the growing number of temporary jobs and among home-workers. The latter are especially common in the poorer peripheral regions of the EU and, in Britain, minority ethnic women are especially likely to be employed in home-working.

Concentrated in poor quality jobs, it is not surprising that women predominate among the ranks of the low paid. In the UK, the Low Pay Unit has drawn attention to the 'strikingly' low level of pay for part-time workers.[17] Black women, even though they are more likely to be in full-time work, are particularly likely to be low paid, as are disabled women.

In all the Member States, with the exception of the UK, women are over-represented among the unemployed.[18] In six countries, female unemployment rates are more than twice male rates. In all but three, female long-term unemployment rates have been rising steadily since 1983. The same phenomenon of high female unemployment is now to be seen in Eastern Europe as women are the first victims of economic restructuring.

The EOC report on the Single European Market (SEM) looked at the prospects for women's employment on a number of different scenarios; under each, it forecast further large increases in the number of part-time jobs with low occupational status and that women are less likely than men to gain from the SEM. Fears have been expressed that the single market will exacerbate women's vulnerable and unprotected patterns of work throughout the EU because they start in a weaker position than men. Jane Pillinger has suggested that, while skilled and mobile women might benefit from more opportunities, unskilled and black and migrant women workers could face diminished rather than expanding opportunities[19]. The vulnerability of those migrant women who are defined as family members and dependants is also emphasised by Gill Whitting.[20]

The economic disadvantage that women face during working life then feeds through into old age. The Final Report of the Second European Poverty Programme noted that among the elderly, poverty tends to be concentrated among women. In the UK, a growing tendency to 'two nations' in old age has been observed, with the poorer nation predominantly female. This tendency could be exacerbated as a growing number of older women are divorced and reliant on inadequate pensions. Women are particularly effected by the fall in the value of the basic state pension relative to average incomes since the indexing link with average earnings was broken in 1980. They are also ill-placed as government policy places increasing emphasis on private pension provision. The gap between the poorer, predominantly female, nation of pensioners and the better off nation is thus likely to widen.

Economic dependency

The importance of women's earnings, and the loss of them through unemployment, sickness or disability, tends to be discounted under the influence of the ideology of women's economic dependency. It is the ideology of women's economic dependency, as much as its actuality, which links women's position in the family and the labour market. At the same time, it helps to obscure the extent to which men are dependent on women for the servicing and care of themselves and their families. As Glendinning and Millar have argued, it does not just describe the economic circumstances of many women, it also legitimates their unequal position inside and outside the home.[21]

In this way, even women who are heads of households or on their own – Afro-Caribbean women, lone parents, lesbians – can still be affected by the ideology, through its effect on their treatment in the labour market, even though they are not economically dependent on a man. In the case of women who are wholly or partially economically dependent on men, this is central to an understanding of their poverty.

The extent of women's economic dependency varies over the life-cycle and between different groups. Thus, for example, Afro-Caribbean women are less likely to be economically dependent than white; disabled women face the constraints imposed by both their gender and a disabling society. Although the trend in most Western European societies has been towards a reduced period of total economic dependency on a male breadwinner's income, it has not been towards genuine economic independence because of the inadequacy of the wages that many women are able to earn.[22] In particular, research indicates that part-time employment generally does not provide a high enough income to enable women to be self-sufficient or to shift the balance of economic power and financial arrangements within households.[23]

Research also points to the importance that many women attach to an independent income from paid employment or social security, especially where it represents an addition to the total family income. A number of studies have indicated that some lone mothers prefer the poverty of lone parenthood to their previous economic position when married to or living with a man because they can exercise greater control over the income that enters the household and how it is then spent.[24] The literature suggests that economic dependence is experienced by many women as a lack of control over resources, a lack of rights and a sense of obligation. This is incompatible with women's status as social citizens which is, in any case, undermined by poverty.[25]

The economist Professor A.B. Atkinson has argued that if one conceives of poverty in terms of a 'right to a minimum level of resources ... we may question whether the dependency of one partner, typically the woman, on the other is acceptable'.[26] This understanding is usually absent from the conceptualisation and measurement of poverty, which is based on the household or family as a unit. Sight is thus lost of the fact that poverty is ultimately experienced by individuals.[27] This is not to deny that poverty is experienced in the context of family and neighbourhood relationships. What it does mean is that one also has to look within the family or household to see how resources are distributed before one can judge whether all the members are or are not in poverty.

There is a growing body of evidence in the UK (I do not know about the rest of Europe) that suggests that resources are not always shared fairly within the family.[28] Particularly striking were the results of a large-scale survey carried out under the Economic and Social Research Council's Social Change and Economic Life initiative. This found that only a fifth of households could be described as egalitarian units in which resources were shared equally.[29]

The unequal intra-household distribution of resources can lead to hidden poverty and either women experiencing poverty more intensely than men or experiencing poverty when their male partners are not because they have only limited access to the latter's income. It is not just a question of the distribution of money but also of the consumption of items such as food and consumer durables. Also, women often sacrifice their own needs in order to try to protect other family members, especially children, from the worst effects of poverty.

Managing and fighting poverty

Furthermore, it tends to be women who manage poverty and debt as part of their general responsibility for money management in low-income families.

This can create stress and affect women's mental and physical health. As the author of a book on women's health and poverty notes:

> For women, the cumulative effect of living in poverty and deprivation mounts up to an array of health hazards, which arise not only from the impact of poverty, and the gender-specific experience of that poverty, but also the nature of the demands made on them in the midst of this deprivation.[30]

Women also tend to act as the main mediators with welfare state institutions, again a stressful activity, especially for black and minority ethnic women, who face potential racism. As the main users (and also providers) of welfare services, women stand to be particularly disadvantaged by cutbacks in and the restructuring of these services.

The management of poverty has to be seen in the context of the point made earlier about women's continued responsibility for the bulk of the unpaid work done in the home, even when they are in paid employment. Research across Europe shows that 'the new man' is hard to find when it comes to the division of unpaid work in the home. He is particularly scarce in Great Britain, Ireland, Southern Spain and Portugal.[31] The burden that this can create for women has led to the coining of the phrase 'time poverty', a concept particularly well known to women in Eastern European countries where women have carried a full burden of paid as well as unpaid work, in conditions of scarcity.

In Denmark, where women's economic activity rates are especially high, time has become a public policy issue, in relation to tackling the stress from combining paid work and family life. Poorer women feel the strains of time poverty most acutely because they cannot 'buy' time in the same way that better-off women can, either through labour-saving devices, or by employing the services of poorer women themselves.

On a more positive note, despite the hard work that poverty spells for women, they are often most active in community-based activities. This can be seen in the Poverty 3 Programme. It also came across very strongly in evidence given to the Opsahl Commission on the way forward for Northern Ireland. The Commission received many examples of how working-class women, both in women's groups and wider community groups, were working within and across communities, to improve conditions and in particular the opportunities open to young people. They formed the mainstay of what Robert D. Puttnam has called the 'capillaries of community life'.[32]

A group of women from North Belfast pointed to how women 'have played a pivotal role in drawing attention to the problems of social and economic deprivation in the area' and a key trust in Northern Ireland drew the Commission's attention to 'the phenomenal contribution of local women's groups in terms of keeping hope alive within and between the divided communities'.[33]

Two quotations from the journal *Poverty* help to illustrate the point further. The first is from a woman contributing to a round-table discussion on women and poverty:

> Being poor has a negative impact on your self-image and self assertiveness. It also saps your energy. There are women on my estate whose expectations have been reduced to the basics of life – that makes me very angry. But there are also women who, despite their poverty, are trying to be assertive. I'm not suggesting that it's a general experience, but there are circumstances that allow women to acknowledge what is happening to them and to build networks of mutual support.[34]

The second is taken from an account of the establishment of a credit union on a Newcastle estate. The majority of the members are women and as one of them put it:

> The women on the estate saw we had a problem so we all got together. There were no arguments, no one-up-man-ship like the kind that happens when men are around. We just decided we needed to do something and we did it.[35]

In the same way, women on a Bradford council estate have spearheaded a campaign against compulsory water-metering which has had an impact nationally. Susan Hyatt, who has documented the campaign, has coined the term 'accidental activism' to describe such 'activism born of the immediate experience of social injustice, rather than as a consequence of a pre-existing ideological belief'. Through such accidental activism, she argues, women, who previously did not see themselves as in any way 'political' are becoming advocates and agents for social change. [36]

Juliet Cook and Shantu Watt have also emphasised the ways in which black women have challenged oppressive structures and processes, together with their resourcefulness in maintaining families and communities under pressure.[37]

Some implications for social security policy

The four key points that I have made about women and poverty – concerning their greater vulnerability to poverty; its structural causes lying in the interrelationship between their position in the family and labour market; hidden female poverty and economic dependency within families; and women's role as the managers of poverty – all have important implications for social security policy. However these implications are all too often ignored in public policy debate.

Considerable progress has been made in removing direct sex discrimination in the operation of social security systems, thanks to EC equal treatment directives. But it has become increasingly clear that equal treatment, defined as the removal of explicit sex discrimination, does not necessarily guarantee equal outcome.

The contributory principle, which is central to the British and many other social security systems, privileges male employment patterns. Women's interrupted employment histories and generally lower earnings put them at a disadvantage. In the UK, two and a quarter million women are officially estimated to be excluded from the contributory system altogether because they earn below the lower earnings limit.

The means-tested income support scheme, upon which about one in six of the total population is now reliant, perpetuates a breadwinner/dependant model, albeit a technically gender-neutral one. Women represent the majority of claimants of most of the major benefits, other than the contributory benefits paid to those below pension age. They are thus more reliant on means-tested benefits and on lower value categorical benefits than on the contributory benefits which were supposed to form the core of the post-war social security scheme. This gendered pattern of benefit receipt has been accentuated by a shift in policy emphasis over the past decade towards greater reliance on means-tested benefits.

The problems with means-tested benefits are well known but the particular disadvantages from the perspective of women's poverty are rarely acknowledged. In couples, even where a means-tested benefit is paid direct to the women, the assessment of eligibility is inevitably based on the couple as the unit. Where income is not shared fairly within families, and as noted already research indicates that often it is not, means-tested benefits can fail to address the hidden poverty that can result. The wider the gap between the assumptions about equitable intra-family income-sharing implicit in mean-testing and the reality, the lower the accuracy of means-tested benefits in targeting help on *individuals* in need. And as argued earlier, it is individuals who ultimately experience poverty and its effects. Means-tested benefits can also be less effective in providing income security at a time of growing instability in family and employment patterns, the consequences of which are experienced particularly harshly by women. Moreover, two of the problems more usually identified with means-testing – low take-up and work disincentives – have gendered dimensions which are insufficiently appreciated. There is some evidence that men, who are reluctant to admit that they cannot support their families without state assistance, are more resistant to claiming means-tested benefits than are women, who have to cope with the everyday consequences of living on an inadequate income. Means-tested benefits can also create a disincentive for the partners of male claimants to take paid work because of the impact on the family's overall income.

The intermittently fashionable notion of some kind of negative income tax, which effectively takes means-testing to its logical conclusion, would institutionalise the couple as the benefit unit at a time when tax systems increasingly take the individual as the tax unit. It would thus represent a major reverse for women's right to be treated as individuals, unless the principle of aggregation were abandoned, which seems very unlikely.

The principle of women's access to social security benefits in their own right is one that has gained wider acceptance in principle in recent years, even if policy developments have been moving in the opposite direction. An ILO report, reviewing the progress made in equality of treatment in social security, noted that:

> Since 1975, increasing emphasis has been placed on the need for all women to have access to social benefits in their own right. Such individual rights are regarded as a decisive factor in achieving equal treatment for men and women in social security.[38]

They have also been seen as giving women greater protection in the face of the increasingly high incidence of family break-up and cohabitation.

Strong support for individual benefit rights has come from the Council of Europe and from the European Parliament. However, a proposal for a further EU social security directive (Com[87]494), which promotes the individualisation of benefits as a means of completing the implementation of equal treatment, has been deferred indefinitely by the Council of Ministers.

The discussion prompted by the Draft Directive focused mainly on the question of derived rights, dependants' allowances and survivors' benefits. These are important questions which need to be approached with care, as recognised by the House of Lords Select Committee on the European Communities which reported on the Draft Directive. There are dangers in introducing reforms in the name of an economic independence which is still, for many women, at best limited. Thus reform, which removes existing protective rights, needs to be gradual.

It also needs to address the more fundamental question as to how social security systems can best guarantee women access to an independent source of income outside the labour market, without at the same time undermining their access to an independent income *through* the labour market. The problem is that the more effective the social security system is in supporting women who are at home providing care, the more likely it is to create a disincentive to them to enter or re-enter the labour market. This could then damage their longer term economic position as well as lock them out of the public sphere more generally, with implications for women's role as citizens.[39]

In Britain the Equal Opportunities Commission has commissioned work on the question.[40] This has looked, in particular, at the potential for reform of the current benefits system. There are a number of incremental reforms which could be made to the system which would improve women's access to an independent income through the benefits system. These would include relaxing (or even abolishing) the contributory principle and the development of existing (or new) contingency benefits paid without either means or contribution test.[41]

More radically, a basic (or citizen's) income scheme would do so by paying a basic benefit to every individual. For many proponents of citizens' income this is one of its main advantages. However, there is a danger, that, without other changes in the labour market and in the division of unpaid caring work between men and women, it might be seen as an encouragement to women to stay at home. It is also doubtful whether a citizen's income, paid without any condition attached, is politically feasible in societies where the work-ethic still has a strong grip and at a time when the Right is placing greater emphasis on the need for strict conditions attached to benefit receipt.

Conclusion

This chapter has set out to make the case for a gendered understanding of poverty. Such an understanding must then be applied to analysis of the social security system and of any reforms proposed to it. If women as individuals are to be effectively protected from poverty, the social security system must be able to direct help to them as individuals. There will be disagreement as to how this is best done and the issue of the individualisation of benefits raises many difficult questions that it has not been possible to explore in this chapter. What is essential is that the principle of women's right to an independent income as full citizens is accepted as a goal of social security and anti-poverty policies.

4 POVERTY, INSTABILITY AND MINIMUM INCOME FOR INTEGRATION (RMI) IN FRANCE

Michel Raymond

Unfortunately, poverty is not a new phenomenon, even in the West. The 'thirty glorious years' of economic growth may have eradicated vast zones of poverty in France but the 1970s and 1980s saw changes in the family, in technology and in the socio-economy which have generated new ones, and we are now seeing a growing instability in society, and the emergence of processes of exclusion.

The Minimum Income for Integration (RMI),[1] established in 1988, has come about because of the increase in these new forms of poverty, and in society's awareness of the problem. Combining a guaranteed minimum income per household with a right to integration and social benefits, the RMI is unquestionably a step forward in social rights and, despite the great disparities between French départements (Departments: administrative regions), the integration programme's results have been significant.

The RMI has limits, however, which have helped to reveal important social dilemmas; what should we prioritise in the fight against exclusion and poverty? Where do those excluded fit in? How are jobs to be provided, activities for people struggling during times of high and growing unemployment? Is there a place for a vast expansion of jobs with a social purpose? What change in our socio-economy and in society itself will enable us to respond quickly, but with long-lasting effect, to structural problems of instability and exclusion.

Poverty, new poverty

Strong and regular economic growth in France during the three decades following the Second World War made considerable economic and social progress possible. The population saw improved standards of living and social protection: retirement benefits, sickness cover, family allowances as well as unemployment benefit. Unemployment was at a low level after the War.

At the beginning of the 1970s, however, traditional areas of poverty still existed, particularly among old or disabled people; this problem was made worse by the rapid disappearance of the extended family which, in the past, had enabled village communities to take care of those in need; but urbanisation, a reduction in the size of homes and the move towards the nuclear family transferred this problem, hitherto a family one, to the social sphere. Lionel Stoleru's *To Vanquish Poverty in Rich Countries*, published at the time, illustrated the type of questions developed societies asked. Nevertheless, the great effort made in the 1970s and up to 1981 to increase the value of the minimum old-age pension,[2] and the establishment of the disabled adult allowance (AAH) in 1975[3] largely enabled these areas of poverty to be eliminated. Simultaneously great changes were taking place on the economic, social and family level which generated new forms of poverty in the 1970s, intensified in the 1980s, where they took on an increasingly international dimension.

The family has been profoundly transformed by various household arrangements succeeding the 'traditional family'. From 1972 to 1973 we saw a decrease in the number of marriages and an increase in the number of divorces and births outside marriage, as well as a growth in the number of single-parent families – mainly single women with one or more children. Some of the latter find themselves with little or no income, but with heavy outgoings (childcare, rent, etc.).

In 1973–4 the oil crisis provided the signal for considerable socio-economic changes: technological progress (electronics, information technology, telecommunications) and the internationalisation of the economy generated a gradual industrial restructuring, an increase in productivity and reduction in the workforce, but also a transformation in jobs, in that an increasingly skilled workforce was required. Unemployment thus grew on a massive scale, reaching 1 million in 1976, 2 million in 1981 and 3 million in 1993.

Loss of a job, a fall in income, debt and sometimes homelessness, family break-up: these factors frequently interact, and the effects accumulate to generate the 'new poverties', an expression used since 1980 by the Oheix Report, an official report published by the Barre government. In addition to poverty, genuine problems of exclusion from society came into play, bringing in their wake social and family difficulties which are intensified in troubled districts of large towns by the problems and errors of town planning, immigration and massive unemployment.

The public authorities reacted with a series of measures: the single-parent allowance in 1977, which today benefits 130,000 single people (principally women) with children; redundancy compensation in 1974; and benefit for the long-term unemployed, with the creation of support payments (ASS) in 1984. In 1984 projects to combat poverty and financial uncertainty were also established.

Awareness of these problems of poverty and exclusion increased, culminating in Father Joseph Wresinski's report to the Economic and Social Council, 'Grande pauvreté et précarité économique et sociale' at the beginning of 1987, with the instigation of local experiments, which have taken place throughout the country, for example in the Departments of Ile-et-Vilaine and Territoire de Belfort.

Minimum income for integration (RMI)

Principles and hopes

From early 1987, the debate gathered momentum. At the end of that year, the socialist group in the National Assembly submitted a bill intended to establish 'a minimum income for integration'.

In 1988 in his 'Letter to the People of France', François Mitterrand, a candidate for the Presidency of the Republic, announced the creation of this minimum income scheme, which aimed to integrate people into the workforce. 'Rights rescue men and women, because they are no longer left abandoned to a power struggle in which they are always the losers' he said in a speech in Montpellier, 19 April 1988. And 'the guaranteed minimum income for integration', will be 'both a sum of money as a result of a recognised right, and a means of restoring dignity with work and an occupation' (Lille, 29 April 1988).

Following his victory in the Presidential election, Mitterrand had his government set about the task of adopting the RMI, with an announcement in the Council of Ministers on 18 May, adoption of the bill in July 1988, an almost unanimous vote in parliament during the autumn. The RMI was established in law on 1 December 1988. The principal decrees were published on 13 December and the law entered into force on 15 December 1988. The exceptional speed with which parliament acted in this case indicates the urgent need for such a measure, despite the country's strong economic growth between 1987 and 1991.

The RMI is based on the following principles:

☐ The right to a minimum income: any person aged at least 25 (or under 25 and responsible for a family) with a very low income is entitled to an allowance which will make up the income to a guaranteed minimum. The sum was originally F2,000 per month for a single person[4] plus F1,000 for the second person in the family, and F600 for the children.

☐ Financing is based on aid at a national level (*solidarité nationale*): it is provided by the state which has delegated the administration of the minimum income allowance to the Family Allowance and the Mutualité Sociale Agricole offices. Overall responsibility is held by the Prefect. The wealth tax, reintroduced at the same time, was the initial source of funding, but now accounts for only one-third of the cost.

☐ Greater social protection: the RMI gives automatic access to basic social rights:

(i) affiliation to a sickness insurance scheme (personal insurance) since the 1988 RMI law for those who had not been entitled to it before. Contributions are financed by the General Council (common law), the family allowance office (person responsible for a family) or the state (homeless people);

(ii) Under the new law about RMI passed on 29 July 1992, additional cover is an automatic right, within the limits of social security tariffs;

(iii) housing benefit (or the APL) at the maximum rate.[5]

☐ The RMI is both a benefit and a right to integration: a right to dignity, to a place in society. 'The integration contract', a particular formula, between the beneficiary and the community, defines the procedures, the objectives and the means provided to achieve this. It has a multi-faceted approach to integration that incorporates social and family life, health, housing, training and employment in order to respond to the inter-related nature of these problems.

The concept of integration is worth examining in more detail, in that it implies the rejection of a system based on assistance.

A localised plan for integration and partnership

The plan for integration into the RMI is conducted entirely at Departmental level, under the joint responsibility of the Prefect and the President of the General Council: the state and the General Council are equal partners, acting in accordance with their decentralised powers to provide jobs and training, public health, housing, state shelter, state social and medical assistance, maternal and child safety (PMI), social services (Department) to which are added compulsory 'integration credits' for the guaranteed minimum income.

Various other bodies or authorities are associated with these two partners, especially at the Departmental level within the Departmental Integration Committee (CDI) and at the local level within the Local Integration Committee (CLI): they include local authorities, associations, employers' federations, housing associations, and Family Allowance and Sickness Assurance offices.

The aim is thus to keep responsibility at the local and Departmental level, and motivate everyone to develop opportunities for integration or reintegration.

Tools for integration

In order to ensure that this development fits in with integration programmes whether Departmental (PDI) or local (PLI), the law of 1988, that of 29 July 1992, and subsequent laws, have laid down various procedures:

(i) compulsory integration credits to be paid by the General Councils[6] and calculated at up to 20 per cent of the previous year's state expenditure for the RMI allowance in that Department. These credits are flexible, but within the integration programme adopted by the Departmental Council (PDI), they enable multiple projects and experiments to be financed. They also usefully complement the state credits, which are generally less flexible, since they are administered at national level.

(ii) measures for employment with, in particular, the 'return to work contract' (CRE) and the 'job creation agreement' (CES) created by the law of 19 December 1989, amended several times.

The 'consolidated job contract' (CEC) created by the law of 29 July 1992 enables jobs to be consolidated over five years with the help of state assistance (exemption from payments of social insurance, unemployment etc. and subsidies averaging 50 per cent). In autumn 1994, Parliament also created 'job contracts for recipients of the RMI', for those in receipt of the RMI and unemployed for at least two years.

These measures, which deal either with obtaining access to the commercial sector (ordinary companies) or the public sector (associations, local authorities and public institutions)[7] are as follows:

□ The law of 31 December 1989 concerning excessive debt, allows difficult situations to be dealt with and the poverty trap avoided.

□ The 'Besson' law of 31 May 1990 concerning the right to housing, making the *'solidarité* fund for housing' (FSL) universal in all Departments, imposing Departmental plans for housing for the most deprived (PDLPD), creating housing-loans to assist integration (PLAI), leases for rehabilitation etc.

□ The Youth Aid Fund (FAY), made universal by the law of 29 July 1992, is available in all Departments to help young people who have difficulty in integrating and thus attempt to avoid their being excluded.

This series of schemes which deal not only with the problem of low income, but also the related areas (health, housing, training, employment etc), raised great hopes of actually attacking serious poverty at source, especially during the period of economic growth 1988–9, creating jobs and encouraging reintegration into the workforce.

Minimum income for integration: first report

Six years after the establishment of the RMI, several lessons can be drawn and some of the risks for society analysed. In particular a National Evaluation Committee for the RMI was established whose report and proposals resulted in the law of 29 July 1992. This modified the RMI scheme and extended the area of the fight against poverty and exclusion, in particular by reforming medical aid and making aid funds available to the young in all Departments.

Most striking is the realisation that a real social need was being answered, judging by the number of people affected and the amounts of money involved and the social dynamics induced.

The number of people involved

The uptake at the end of 1988 and early 1989 was rapid, but the numbers continued to grow significantly each year: the economy continued to produce marginalisation, even in periods of growth, but especially during the slackening in the economy and the recession of 1993. Unemployment, the major source of poverty and exclusion, was not reduced.

Table 4.1 People Receiving the RMI

	Number of recipients[a] at the end of the year[b]	% annual increase
1989	335,000	–
1990	422,000	+25.7%
1991	488,000	+16.2%
1992	575,000	+17.8%
1993	697,000	+21.2%
1994	833,000[c]	+19.5%[c]

[a] not including Overseas Departments, where the situation appears to have been stable, mainly owing to the policy of setting the same level of family allowances as on the mainland, with an increase in 1994: 1989: 91,100; 1990: 88,000; 1991: 94,000; 1992: 96,200; 1993: 96,300; 1994: 107,000 (+11%)
[b] National statistics only count the number of people actually receiving the RMI; people whose income temporarily exceeds the guaranteed minimum level are not included
[c] provisional estimate (France)

Including the Overseas Departments, approximately 940,000 households received the RMI at the end of 1994. In the six years since the introduction of the RMI more than 1,700,000 households, representing almost 3.5 million people with spouses and children, will have been helped. This is a substantial number, showing the extent of the need. It also shows, and this is fundamental, that a large number of the recipients have left the scheme.

Who receives the RMI?

What kind of person benefits from RMI? Is there a typical recipient?

There are, in fact, a variety of people who participate in RMI, from the young who are marginalised (but also some who are unemployed after finishing their studies) to the older unemployed person, to those retired with insufficient entitlement to a retirement pension (e.g. a retired person who is under 65 or a foreigner) through to women alone following a family break-up, and with no work experience outside the home.

If we were to be contentious, might we say that all those not included in these categories are tramps or even, as is sometimes said, profiteers? Might they also just be lazy, content to let society take care of them? The reality is quite different: those outside the above categories are mainly long-term unemployed, with low levels of training or qualifications. Their first request after a minimum income is a job, even if it is from a job creation scheme which only brings in half the statutory minimum wage. Many also have difficulties with health or housing, which must be resolved.

On average the participants receive F1,837 per month guaranteed minimum income, a very modest income level, which makes it difficult to solve the problems they encounter. This is particularly true in gaining access to housing (despite the various housing benefits), although this is a basic requirement for long-term integration.

The main characteristics of recipients of the RMI are:

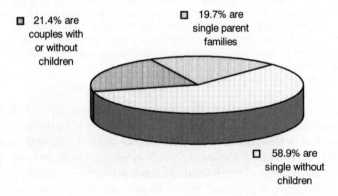

◩ 21.4% are couples with or without children

▫ 19.7% are single parent families

▫ 58.9% are single without children

• Single people are in the majority

Poverty, Instability and Minimum Income in France

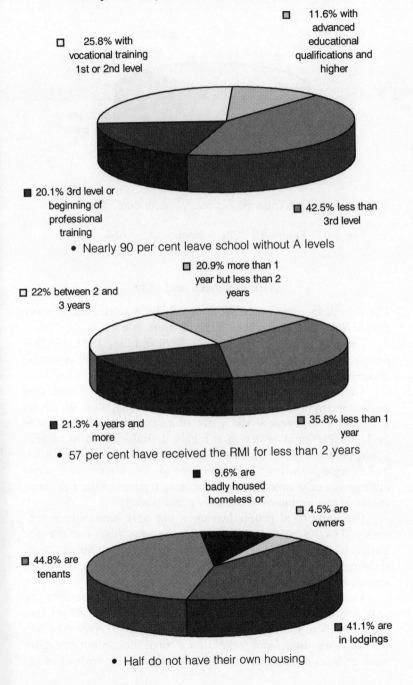

☐ 25.8% with vocational training 1st or 2nd level

▨ 11.6% with advanced educational qualifications and higher

▨ 20.1% 3rd level or beginning of professional training

▨ 42.5% less than 3rd level

- Nearly 90 per cent leave school without A levels

▨ 20.9% more than 1 year but less than 2 years

☐ 22% between 2 and 3 years

▨ 21.3% 4 years and more

▨ 35.8% less than 1 year

- 57 per cent have received the RMI for less than 2 years

■ 9.6% are badly housed homeless or

☐ 4.5% are owners

▨ 44.8% are tenants

▨ 41.1% are in lodgings

- Half do not have their own housing

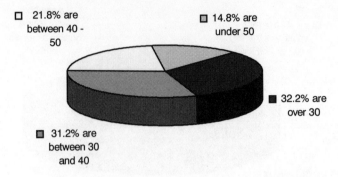

☐ 21.8% are between 40 - 50

☐ 14.8% are under 50

☐ 32.2% are over 30

☐ 31.2% are between 30 and 40

- A third are under 30 but nearly 15 per cent are over 50

Figure 4.2   Characteristics of the RMI

RMI: entrances and exits

The overall increase in the workforce hides a stark reality: many people leave the RMI scheme but still more join.

For the 12 months between June 1993 and June 1994, 184,000 people were recorded as leaving the scheme, but 319,000 as joining (figures CAF France).

Those joining the scheme have been victims of the exclusion process inherent in the structure of French society, with, no doubt, a further component – the years of recession – adding to the problem. Preventative action is highly desirable, both as regards young people who are nearing 25 and in danger of marginalisation, and as regards the long-term unemployed. The massive and growing number of people joining the scheme testifies to the enormous extent of the problems of instability and poverty.

The number of people leaving is not only increasing significantly (184,000 against 154,000 the previous year) but the rate has been maintained despite the unfavourable economic situation, showing that the attempts at reintegration are working as regards employment, as well as in health and housing.

The rate of people leaving the scheme is 30 per cent after one year, and more than 50 per cent after two. More than 70 per cent of recipients in the first year of the scheme (1989) have now left. However, we should not forget that a small though not negligible number from each group is still in the scheme: for reasons of age

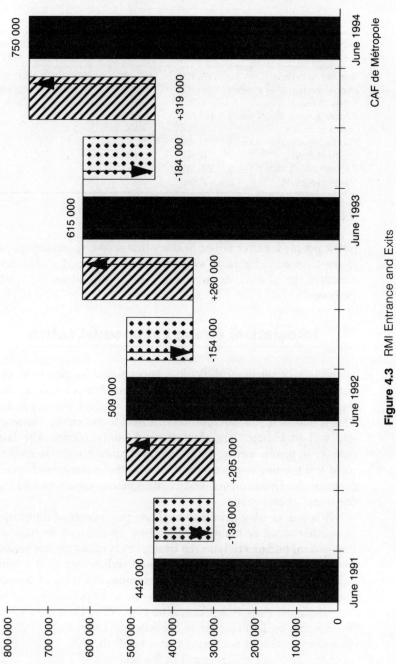

Figure 4.3 RMI Entrance and Exits

Table 4.4   People Leaving RMI

joined	1st half 1989	2nd half 1989	1990	1st half 1991
Number of people	336,700	107,400	192,100	100,000
People leaving after 2 years	159,700	56,000	103,800	53,200
rate of leaving	47%	52%	54%	53%
People leaving after 3 years	191,500	68,600	121,7000	
rate of leaving	57%	64%	63%	
People leaving after 4 years	217,400	76,700		
rate of leaving	65%	71%		
People leaving after 5 years	236,200			
rate of leaving	70%			

Sector: CAF de Métropole
Source: DIRMI from CNAF figures

(some people are over 60) or health – that is to say, reasons specific to the individual, but from which we can also generalise. This level indicates the absence or inadequacy of opportunities for reintegration.

Integration: strong but unequal action

In the face of the great difficulties encountered by people in situations of poverty and exclusion (the descent is much quicker than the climb back up to a 'normal' life), there has been positive action. This is thanks to the mobilisation of a new-found public awareness and will to change, large budgets and human effort. The large number of people leaving the scheme and gaining access to employment and training testify to this. However this is not spread equally between the Departments, and is still not enough overall to stop the spiral of exclusion.

It is not an easy matter to evaluate the success of integration as regards social or family life (bringing up children, managing a family mini-budget etc.) or even health (legal rights are not enough to guarantee proper access to care and well-being) as it is difficult to quantify. We can, however, examine the areas of housing and integration into working life.

Access to housing

The award of housing allowance at the maximum rate, as a right deriving from the RMI, has enabled thousands of recipients to gain access to housing, or rehousing in a modified scheme. There have even been experiments such as estate agencies specialising in social housing. Progress has been seen overall in housing; however half of the recipients did not have a home of their own.

It must be said that the housing market is extremely selective, and difficult for people with low or very low incomes; housing bodies, struggling with their administrative difficulties, are rarely prepared to enter the fray; and collective will (apart from that of the author-sponsor of the 'Besson' law) is largely lacking both at the national and the local level, other than in the provision of shelters for the homeless (SDF) during the winter.

Beyond the conventional speeches, and moving appeals from Abbé Pierre,[8] a collective jolt is needed in this vital area of housing, where associations (and some local authorities and a few housing bodies) are often the driving force, using private housing. Is there a future in the use of requisition, as advocated by the Mayor of Paris? And will this compensate for market forces which have been in place for years?

Incentives, such as the taxation of housing deliberately left vacant, could result in thousands of existing flats and houses coming on to the market. Concurrently, there must be an effort to build state housing for rent, whilst ensuring that the level of rent remains low enough for those on low incomes to afford.

Integration into working life

It is worth noting that, of the employment and training to which 240,000 people have gained access, approximately half is in the public sector, with job creation contracts and 'consolidated employment'. This shows the considerable scope for job creation in the public utility sector: a promising sign, given the shortage of long-term employment opportunities for people in difficulty in a period of growing unemployment.

We must stress, however, that the proportion of recipients of the RMI gaining access to employment or training decreased in 1993 (32.5 per cent compared to 36 per cent in 1992) and again

Figure 4.5 Integration into Working Life

	1993	1994[1]	94/93
Vacancies filled, not covered by assisted contracts	42,000	46,000	+9.5%
New companies established	3,000	3,500	+16.7%
Agent associations and integration companies	8,000	9,000	+12.5%
Return to work contract (CRE)	14,800	21,500	+45.3%
Subtotal, commercial sector	67,800	80,000	+18.0%
Job creation contract (CES) (initial agreements)	93,100	107,000	+14.9%
Consolidated job contract (CEC) (initial agreements)	3,000	7,000	+133.0%
Sub total, non commercial sector	96,100	114,000	+18.6%
Total access to employment	163,000	194,000	+18.4%
Access to training (SIFE)	42,250	46,000	+8.9%
TOTAL	206,150	240,000	+16.4%

[1] provisional estimate on the basis of the first nine months of 1994

slightly in 1994 (31.2 per cent), owing to the very rapid increase in the number of recipients.

Geographical disparities and inequalities in integration

There are great disparities between Departments, if we judge using criteria such as access to integration in working life, or the take-up of integration credits.

Local differences, particularly with regard to the economy and employment, only partly explain this. More significant are factors such as the determination of local participants, the distribution of skills, and existence of strong local networks: attributable to local tradition.

These disparities among the regions and lack of equal opportunities for the recipients of the RMI, in particular in the Parisian region and around the Mediterranean, are quite unacceptable.

The role of the state has been, and still is, essential as a guarantor of national unity and fairness. Otherwise how many towns or Departments would be content with providing a minimum wage without any form of integration, i.e. providing assistance but at the same time retaining the exclusion factor?

Table 4.6 Geographical Disparities and Inequalities in Integration

	France	Average of the ten 'best' (A)	National average	Average of the ten 'least good' (B)	Ratio between A and B
Workforce	Density of RMI (number per 10,000 habitants)	62	123	196	3.2
	Rate of growth 1993	8.9%	21.1%	38.4%	4.3
Integration	Integration credits disbursed in 1993 per paid beneficiary	F5,049	F3,087	F2,258	2.2
	Rate of integration contract[1]	102%	47.3%	14%	7.3
Access to employment and training	Rate of access to CES	29%	14.3%	6.3%	4.6
	Rate of access to CRE	3.9%	2.1%	1.2%	3.3
	Rate of access to AIF	11.5%	6.7%	3.2%	3.6
	Overall rate CES + CRE + AIF[2]	40.8%	23.1%	13.9%	2.9

NB: the ten 'best' or the ten 'least good' are not the same for each criterion.
[1] The denominator does not include the 'pending' recipients, the ratio may be greater than 100 per cent
[2] This overall rate is not the sum of the three previous ones

The financial risks

It is difficult to draw up an exact balance sheet, if only because a recipient of the RMI may also be long-term unemployed, and it would be difficult to determine in which category this cost should be recorded. A summary balance sheet has been drawn up with estimates for 1994, by recording the direct costs relating to the RMI.

The state, an essential source of finance

In the name of national solidarity, the state provides the basic funding for the RMI: principal expenditure is on the provision of the minimum income, but half of the expense of the integration programme is also covered.

Table 4.7 Development of the Two Principal Items of State Expenditure for RMI (in billions of francs)

	1989	1990	1991	1992	1993	1994
RMI	6.23	10.27	12.15	13.92	16.34	19.5[a]
Employment measures (CRE, CES and CEC, AIF and SIFE, ACCRE)	1.0	2.6	2.9	3.42	3.85	4.85[a]

[a] provisional estimate

Several other types of state expenditure must be added to these two principal items, which totalled 24.35 billion in 1994: state integration credits for the Overseas Departments ('credit' making up the lowest level of the RMI) of F750 million in 1994, management credits of F250 million, specific to the RMI (decentralised credits Chapter 37.13.20 of the Departmental health agency, DDASS, on the one hand, Social Affairs, budgetary items and the national employment agency [ANPE] created for the RMI on the other); also the increase in housing aid to those entitled to it, approximately F850 million, giving a direct total for the state of more than F26 million in 1994, which in current circumstances can only increase. This direct cost can be added to in various ways, through ordinary schemes, housing assistance, temporary housing centres, social housing funds, and state medical assistance for homeless people, for example.

The General Councils, the second source of income

The law imposes two financial obligations on the General Councils:

Integration credits

These amount to 20 per cent of state expenditure on RMI payments in the previous year in the Department: these credits are still disbursed unequally; some Departments generally exceed the legal

Table 4.8 State Expenditure on RMI Payments (in millions of francs)

1989	1990	1991	1992	1993	1994
269	807	1,434	2,079	2,545	3,100[a]

[a] provisional estimate

obligation, others are still far from doing so (under the law any credits not disbursed must be carried over).

Sickness cover

This is medical assistance, including the financing of the personal contribution, for those without medical cover and not belonging to the CAF (family allowance fund) or the state homelessness (SDF) schemes, and additional cover (including crisis payments).

This 100 per cent sickness cover is therefore normally guaranteed to any recipient. The personal cover is a specific financial obligation on the part of the General Councils, and the additional cover is partly financed through integration credits.[9]

The overall cost (with deduction of the calculation for integration credits) is estimated at F2.4 billion for 1993 and F2.8 billion for 1994.

These two types of expenditure represent a gross cost for the General Councils. In fact, when the RMI was established, they saved money on their assistance and social action (particularly on assistance in childcare and local additions to resources) whilst they were already financing most of the sickness cover through the medical assistance scheme.

During a parliamentary discussion in 1988 it was estimated that the transactions were balanced, more or less. This is no longer the case, given the doubling of the RMI in four years, and the net cost is doubtless somewhere between 3.5 and 4 billion francs.

A balance sheet of F32 Billion in 1994 and growing fast

The state therefore covers 82 per cent of the direct cost of the RMI, as part of its duty to guarantee national solidarity.

It goes without saying that other participants (such as local authorities, family allowance offices, associations) also provide assistance and volunteers, but this is difficult to quantify and clearly less significant.

Table 4.9 Expenditure on RMI and Related Costs, 1994

	State	General Councils	TOTAL
RMI payments	19.50		
Employment measures	4.85		
DOM integration credits	0.75		
Direct management costs	0.25		
Housing assistance increase	0.85		
Integration credits		3.1	
Personal insurance and medical assistance	2.8		
TOTAL	26.20	5.9	32.10
in %	81.6%	18.4%	

The dramatic increase in this expenditure, even if it 'only' represents 1.5 per cent of the total expenditure on social protection, undoubtedly poses a problem: both in itself as it must be financed, but also and especially as an indicator of the growing problems of exclusion.

Instability, poverty, exclusion: structural processes of exclusion

An analysis of developments over 20 years shows the rise of a process of exclusion which can be interpreted as structural in origin. In fact this tendency is long term and powerful, and the processes are cumulative.

Changes in the economy hardly affect the deep-rooted character of this phenomenon; this is most particularly true in the field of employment where, following the recession, the growth experienced in 1995, however desirable and positive this may be, will very largely be illusionary for the most deprived: the two-tier society will be accentuated.

There are four types of exclusion which are interconnected and cumulative, leaving aside specific factors such as immigration, deprived areas, etc.

Exclusion by unemployment

This is a major factor of exclusion as it not only involves a drop and then a loss of income, but also a feeling of uselessness to society. It has multiple causes that have existed for some 20 years; we can only give the principal causes:

☐ New technologies in information, electronics and telecommunications, taking us towards the 'information superhighway', and boosted by the effects of the oil crisis of 1973–4, have brought about a true technological revolution in products, and in the production process. Gains in productivity have been considerable both in the traditional sectors (the car industry, for example) and in the tertiary sector, where development will be even more rapid in the years to come.

☐ The internationalisation and the globalisation of the economy are an incontrovertible reality, resulting in a race for productivity on a world scale in order to compete. Much more than the relocation of companies which has affected certain sectors (though the French balance of trade is bearing up well, so there is no major danger on this point), it is this need to stay competitive which imposes major limits on employment.

☐ The specific demography of France (the difference between young people arriving on the job market and those retiring, the increased rate of female activity) means an increase in the working population from 150,000 to 180,000 people per year, requiring the creation of as many jobs simply to maintain the present level of unemployment.

☐ The gap between types of jobs and qualifications; technology today means more qualifications are required for jobs. Yet a section of the population has a low or very low level of qualification, owing either to age (unemployed former semi-skilled workers), or to personal difficulties. In addition, even for jobs requiring no or few qualifications, employers tend to recruit qualified people.

Even if other factors (such as heavy costs) play their part in the difficulties, these principal causes form the heart of the exclusion process at the employment level.

Instability is increasing – unemployment is following its disastrous evolution: 1995 will no doubt produce the illusion of a slight decrease in unemployment owing to strong growth, in the order of 3 per cent; but the experts[10] put the rate of increase required simply to stabilise the rate of unemployment at 2.7 per cent: I quote from page 25 of the Maarek report *Documentation Française*:

> Faced with the average forecast of institutes of the order of 2.5 per cent (annual economic growth up to the year 2000), concerning equally the trend of 2.3 per cent observed over twenty years, this figure of 2.7 per cent gives us reason to fear a continuation in the progression of unemployment.

There are several indications which enable this break-up of our society (and of other Western societies, plus Japan, with, of course, elements applicable to each one) to be analysed:

(i) the increase in instability in employment, with the multiplication of temporary work and the introduction of fixed-length contracts.

(ii) changes in unemployed people's progress during this period of economic recovery:

- the number of unemployed almost stable (in one year) — 3,334,200[11] +1.4 per cent

- the number of short-term unemployed (less than one year) — 2,109,200 −5.3 per cent

- the number of long-term unemployed (more than one year) — 1,225,000 +15.6 per cent

- the growth of the RMI (France) in 1994 — 833,000 +19.6 per cent

- but also rapid development in the preceding years, including those with high economic growth (1989–92): +25.7 per cent in 1990; +15.7 per cent in 1991; +17.7 per cent in 1992; +21.1 per cent in 1993.

- the divergence between the overall growth of unemployment and the receipt of benefit: 3,334,800 unemployed (+1.4 per cent in one year) against 1,892,800 unemployed receiving benefit from the unemployment insurance scheme (UNEDIC), that is −5.5 per cent, whilst the unemployment solidarity level, which is lower and reserved for the long-term unemployed, has seen its numbers sharply increase: 453,600, that is +13.8 per cent.

(iii) the rapid decrease in the level of unemployment benefits with the creation of the single decreasing allowance (AUD) in 1992; giving 82 per cent of unemployed people receiving benefit of less than F5,000 per month, 46.3 per cent less than F3,000, whilst approximately one million unemployed received no benefit, including almost 500,000 young people.

(iv) almost one million people are in temporary schemes and receive little (or very little) benefit. This is particularly true of job creation schemes (417,000 people receiving a half SMIC [national minimum wage] i.e. just under F2,500 per month), training, conversion or pre-retirement courses (FNE [National Employment Fund]).

These factors show the extent of the problem for our society and therefore the need for concerted action.

Exclusion for family reasons

The 'family' went through major upheaval from the beginning of the 1970s and this has had serious repercussions in terms of instability, and of poverty and exclusion.

The number of marriages (280,000) dropped by a third, whilst the number of divorces climbed to more than 100,000; the number of single-parent families grew considerably, going from 847,000 in 1982 to 1,350,000 in 1990 (+59 per cent), 86 per cent of these parents being women, with more than 130,000 receiving single-parent allowances (guaranteed minimum for one or three years, a little higher than the RMI).

The fragility of relationships between couples, and the financial, organisational and also psychological difficulties of single people in charge of families are at the heart of this exclusion process, especially as the situation is frequently compounded by problems with housing, training, employment and income.

Exclusion by housing

As stated already, the urban housing market is selective. Many other factors are added to the mechanisms of the market, and these lead to exclusion: the lack of sufficient state housing particularly in town centres; the reduction in people leaving social housing either for the private rental sector or to acquire property; in addition, the maintenance in HLM (low-cost, state-owned housing) for families whose income exceeds the ceiling for subsidised housing, without this 'subsidised income' systematically becoming an element of financial compensation.

In the private sector, the guarantees demanded by owners make it more and more difficult for families of average income to gain access, whilst much housing remains intentionally vacant and thus tax exempt.

Added to these general factors for people on low or very low incomes is an almost insoluble contradiction, that of excessive rents, including those found in subsidised housing (particularly because of improvements in standards), in relation to the financial limits for housing assistance. The current measures (such as loans for tenants to assist in integration or highly subsidised loans, the PLAI and PLATS) do not solve the problem. There is a need to rethink housing policy to produce, both in new and old housing, accommodation with a sufficiently 'moderate' rent to be truly accessible to people on the lowest incomes.

Exclusion by health

The law of 29 July 1992 provided for sickness cover of 100 per cent automatically given to people on the RMI scheme. In addition it granted the right to personal sickness insurance for young people with little means (up to the level of the RMI), and reformed the medical assistance scheme which was more than a century old.

But the reality is different because of the complexity of the procedures, conflicts between the appropriate authorities (notably between the state and the General Council), and the link between sickness insurance and medical assistance.

These administrative difficulties hamper the systematic provision of free health care at a time of real health problems. The combination of marginalisation, family and social break-up, the experience of isolation and a loss of identity and dignity are factors that contribute to ill-health and may lead to alcoholism and mental breakdown.

These four processes of interconnected and accumulating exclusion make up a structural problem which society must treat as such.

Two major risks for society

The structured process of exclusion and the formation of a two-tier society pose a danger to society in themselves, but the manner of the response is also potentially dangerous.

The RMI, which has been of enormous benefit to 1,700,000 households in six years, has also dramatically revealed the problems of poverty and mechanisms of exclusion. The RMI has also been the driving force behind new schemes for integration which in themselves raise new issues.

The first potentially dangerous area concerns the problem of what priority society will give to the fight against poverty and exclusion, and for integration. Is it going to be content with paying a minimum wage to an ever-increasing number of recipients? Is it going to drive recipients away by requesting further qualifications or by limiting their entitlements? Or is it really going to try to eradicate the problems of exclusion from our developed societies? Is it ready to add 10 or 20 billion francs, that is 0.5 per cent to 1 per cent of social security expenditure, to tackle the root causes and really organise itself to prevent exclusion and to activate integration?

For beyond the 'sensational' which is represented for the media and for politicians (and consequently for public opinion) by the death of a tramp in winter, it must be stated that poverty, and therefore the poor, leaves many people largely indifferent, be they decision-makers (at a national or local level) or simply 'citizens'. The poor and the disadvantaged have not, or with very few exceptions, chosen to be so. Our rich and developed society will be judged on the fate it accords them in the future.

The second difficult task for an adult society is how to integrate a growing number of disadvantaged people successfully into a society, into an internationalised and productive economy which generates more and more unemployment, except during rare years of solid growth. Should an economic policy be followed by growth and a reduction in working hours, who believes that this alone would really be a solution for the future? It represents a vast problem in terms of reorganisation, and an indispensable redistribution of wealth and of activities.

In particular, knowing the strong constraints of the traditional commercial sector (in the current climate, employers will never take on more people than required to meet demand), the risk is to create new, similar jobs, in particular in socially useful areas, where there could be a net creation of jobs on a massive scale for activities and services valuable to the community, and for which the local authorities, associations and public establishments do not currently have sufficient resources.

This is a whole strategy to convert passive expenditure (such as unemployment payments and RMI subsidies) into active expenditure for employment and use by society, and which can actually be implemented.

The existence of 400,000 job creation contracts (CES) in France demonstrates that the demand is there. The 25,000 consolidated employment contracts signed in two years (contracts exempt from charges and subsidised over five years by the state) confirm, despite their imperfections, that CES-type jobs can be transformed into long-term employment.

Outside France various countries have similar schemes and some have gone even further. Denmark, for instance, has just established an obligation for local authorities to propose action for integration.

Today, alongside measures intended to encourage a return to a spirit of enterprise (such as the return to work contract, and the RMI work contract) or the creation of new activities (such as assistance to an unemployed person setting up a company), the time has come to create socially useful jobs for the workforce, by organising the re-using of public and community funds for long-term, properly paid, jobs enabling various struggling sectors of the population to find their place and their dignity in society.

Society's other interests lie in access to housing, and real and easy access to care for the most deprived. Changing the housing policy and simplifying legislation for sickness cover are, in principle, much easier to achieve even if the many forms of selfishness, at national and local level, do their utmost to demolish these elementary rights.

At the end of the twentieth century, when so much economic and social progress has been achieved, we are surprised at the increase in the instances of poverty, instability and exclusion. They correspond to a transformation in the nature of society, the economy and technology. Let us learn to hasten progress in ideas and positive decisions, so that the national wealth benefits everyone and that instability, poverty and exclusion become a decreasing trend.

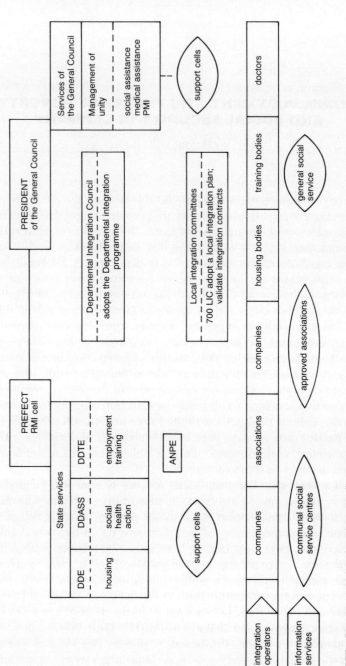

Figure 4.10 Departmental and Local Integration Scheme

DDTE – Departmental job and employment office
DDASS – Departmental health and social services office

93

5 UNEMPLOYMENT, THE THREAT OF POVERTY, AND SOCIAL SECURITY IN GERMANY

Wolfgang Schütte

European welfare states will only be able to meet the challenge of 'new-age poverty' if governments are prepared to combat increasingly widespread marginalisation trends. Measures to combat mass unemployment play a vital part in this. Roger Lawson reaches the same conclusion in his authoritative, in-depth report. He highlights the implications of the most recent economic crises in an international comparison.[1] Current job market trends and political policies designed to contain these trends in Germany reveal how this challenge is being met in practice. Lawson's proposals are currently being hampered by supply-oriented economic policy. They are also being held back by the problem of inertia within the social security system. This system was devised during a period of comparatively stable job market conditions and family relationships. It is now threatening to obstruct essential restructuring initiatives. Finally, there is the question of the future and whether the role of the welfare state needs to be redefined in the face of the increasingly fragmented world of work, where a policy designed to eradicate poverty could be more successful.

I suspect that European social security systems will be gradually forced to move away from the idea of being able to influence social inequality. A policy to eradicate poverty which is designed to encompass the concept of 'social citizenship' in two ways could achieve this. First, by providing basic economic security (with comprehensive vocational training and guidance) and second, by giving local, individual assistance with professional reintegration.

The current job market crisis in Germany is highlighted below in the context of this brief case study on the basis of a number of key statistics (see Job Market Crisis, p. 95). These reveal a number of parallels for victims threatened by poverty (see Unemployment and the Threat of Poverty, p. 98). Subsequently, a series of measures

94

within the German social security system are described which are designed to prevent unemployment from being inextricably linked with poverty (see Social Security and its Shortcomings, p. 99). The social security system in Germany is mainly funded via contributions. Its capacity is therefore always stretched to the utmost just when it is needed most. Official social policy tends to get caught up in a maze of conflicting political concepts. Social policy is always seen as a necessary evil in conservative supply-oriented economic policy, like the one currently supported by the ruling parliamentary parties. Unemployment benefit was originally based on a number of key objectives which were designed to eradicate poverty, and the future of these is now being questioned in the debate on basic principles in social policy (see German Social Policy Response, p. 103).

There is clearly great uncertainty behind the day-to-day political disputes on allocation and budget debates. Numerous fundamental issues in social security are being reviewed in the light of the current crisis. They include the relationship between incentives and controls, a minimum level of income and benefits, active and passive labour market policy, etc. The lively, innovative debate on *how* we are to move towards 'social citizenship' in social policy still has a long way to go (see Open Questions, p. 104).

Job market crisis in Germany

In the international arena, the (former) FRG was in the bottom third in terms of unemployment and like nations up to 1990. If you exclude Japan and Scandinavia and the smaller neighbouring countries, such as Switzerland, Holland, Luxembourg and Denmark, the German job market looked *relatively* flexible even in times of recession. Compared to the EC average, West Germany still only had 50–60 per cent unemployment in the 1970s and 1980s by comparison. This still applies in the former FRG states today (see Table 5.1).

Since reunification in 1990 and the most recent crisis in the industrialised West, this rough outline no longer presents a true picture of the German job market. Unemployment figures in West Germany rose again sharply in 1992 following the four-year boom: this time as a result of relatively high unemployment with 1.7 million out of work and the hangover from the structural crisis of

Table 5.1 Unemployment Levels (as a Percentage of the Total Workforce): International Comparisons

Country	1970–1980	1980–1990	1990	1991	1992	1992 July	Aug	Sept	Oct	Nov	Dec	1993 Jan	Feb	Mar	April	May
Belgium	4.6	10.4	7.6	7.5	8.2	8.2	8.3	8.3	8.4	8.5	8.6	8.8	8.9	9.1	9.2	9.4
Germany[a]	2.5	5.7	4.8	4.2	4.5	4.6	4.6	4.6	4.8	4.8	4.9	5.0	5.1	5.3	5.4	5.5
Denmark	4.3	7.4	8.1	8.9	9.5	9.7	9.6	9.6	9.6	9.8	10.0	9.9	9.9	10.0	10.4	10.6
Finland	3.7	4.7	3.4	7.6	13.1	12.8	13.6	13.2	14.4	15.3	15.4	16.6	18.0	17.4	17.7	16.7
France	4.1	9.0	9.0	9.5	10.0	10.1	10.0	10.1	10.1	10.2	10.3	10.3	10.4	10.5	10.6	10.7
Greece	2.4	6.7	7.2	7.7	7.7	—	—	—	—	—	—	—	—	—	—	—
Britain	3.8	9.5	7.0	9.1	10.8	10.8	11.0	11.1	11.2	11.3	11.5	11.5	11.4	11.4	11.4	11.4
Ireland	7.0	15.2	14.5	16.2	17.8	18.0	18.1	18.3	18.2	18.4	18.3	18.4	18.5	18.4	18.4	18.6
Italy	6.5	9.3	10.0	10.0	10.1	10.2	10.2	10.4	10.3	10.3	10.6	10.6	10.1	10.4	10.6	10.7
Japan	1.7	2.5	2.1	2.1	2.2	2.2	2.2	2.2	2.3	2.3	2.4	2.3	2.3	2.3	2.3	2.5
Canada	6.7	9.2	8.1	10.2	11.2	11.6	11.6	11.3	11.3	11.7	11.4	11.0	10.8	11.0	11.3	11.3
Luxembourg	0.3	2.5	1.7	1.6	1.9	1.9	2.0	2.1	2.0	2.0	2.1	2.0	2.1	2.4	2.5	2.5
Holland	3.9	9.9	7.5	7.0	6.7	6.1	6.4	6.6	7.0	7.1	7.0	7.2	7.6	7.8	7.9	—
Norway	1.1	3.0	5.2	5.5	5.4	6.1	5.8	5.0	4.8	4.9	5.5	6.1	5.8	5.6	5.6	5.1
Austria	1.8	4.2	5.4	5.8	5.9	4.6	4.8	5.0	5.8	6.5	7.7	8.4	8.2	7.3	6.9	6.2
Portugal	5.0	7.1	4.6	4.1	4.8	4.7	4.8	4.7	4.7	4.8	4.9	5.0	5.2	7.1	7.7	7.5
Sweden	2.1	2.4	1.5	2.7	4.8	5.3	5.8	5.2	5.2	5.4	5.5	7.5	7.3	4.9	5.0	4.6
Switzerland	0.4	0.6	0.6	1.3	3.0	2.9	3.1	3.3	3.5	3.9	4.2	4.6	4.8	4.9	5.0	4.6
Spain	5.2	17.9	16.1	16.3	18.0	18.1	18.1	18.3	18.9	19.3	19.6	20.0	20.4	21.0	20.7	21.0
USA	6.2	7.0	5.5	6.7	7.4	7.6	7.5	7.4	7.3	7.2	7.2	7.0	6.9	6.9	6.9	6.8
EC	4.2	9.3	8.3	8.7	9.5	9.5	9.6	9.7	9.8	9.9	10.0	10.1	10.2	10.3	10.4	10.5

Source: EC Statistical Office, International Labour Office, OECD. Calculations are based on seasonally adjusted international estimates.
The latest figures are provisional figures
(a) Former FRG states

the 1980s. Unemployment at the end of 1993/94 (2.5 million) accounted for just over 8 per cent. In East Germany, the figure was over 15 per cent, with 1.2 million registered unemployed.

Yet, the real situation is not adequately reflected in these figures.

☐ Over 80,000 of the unemployed, who are 58 years of age or more, are considered unemployable. Consequently, they do not figure in the statistics.

☐ Over 600,000 unemployed people have taken early retirement from the age of 55. They are not officially classed as unemployed either.

☐ Almost 400,000 receive a wage from the German Employment Office as a result of job creation schemes. These are short-term, government-funded jobs in the 'secondary job market' (over 300,000 of which are in East Germany).

☐ Well over 600,000 jobless people also take part in government-funded vocational training schemes

☐ And up to 1.7 million account for the so-called 'hidden reserves', consisting of those who have no entitlement to benefit, and are not therefore registered with the German Employment Office.

A further 3.4 million from the unofficial figures therefore have to be added to the 3.7 million from the official unemployment figures to gain some idea of the job crisis affecting Germany as a whole. With a potential workforce of 38.7 million, this produces an unemployment rate of 18.4 per cent.

It is important these unemployment figures are shown in context, i.e. against the background of the economic crisis which has affected the entire industrialised West since the end of the 1980s. The FRG remains in a comparatively favourable position. Opening up the borders to the East increased demand, and consequently, there were no marked signs of crisis before 1992 in Germany. On the other hand, the German job market has been particularly hard hit in the medium and long term. The vast majority of the industrial conglomerates in the East have since collapsed. Most were unable to compete in the deregulated Common Market with their low levels of productivity and inferior product quality. This process of de-industrialisation is ongoing. Unprofitable operations are still being artificially boosted by state subsidies. It is impossible to say at this stage whether access to the Eastern markets will have the desired compensatory effect, as the underlying political stability required for growth-oriented trading relations is not yet in place.

The process of de-industrialisation in the East is taking place at a time of economic recession in the industrialised nations and with the impact of German reunification. The third important factor shaping economic policy at this time is *structural change* which is expected to affect industrialised core member states throughout Europe. Industrial nations in Central Europe will also have to face production plant losses, and consequently, further job cuts in industry in future with more global division of labour. Construction of international transport routes and channels of communication will favour threshold nations which will be able to profit from their world market advantage over established industrialised nations with their relatively low production costs.

Regional reports confirm how little information average statistics of this nature provide. In the Ueckermark district, in the far north east of unified Germany, for example, one in two workers are unemployed according to the statistics. Men and women over 50 have no prospect of finding a permanent job in the medium term. The psychosocial consequences can be seen in the women's refuges, which are filled to capacity, and the dramatic fall in the birth rate. No prospects and fear of the future are leading to greater family and personal problems, including stress, depression and addiction according to local social services reports.[2]

Unemployment and the threat of poverty

Unemployment is always seen as a major conducive factor in any assessment of the specific threat of poverty. All studies on poverty concur that there is a direct link between exclusion clauses and requirements for professional integration, and structural problems affecting the poor.

This is characterised by a number of statistics.

☐ Supplementary benefit is the lowest means-tested benefit in the social security system. In statistics, unemployment is always given as the main reason for claiming supplementary benefit (West Germany: 33 per cent of all cases monitored, East Germany: 67 per cent).[3]

☐ Studies of real household income show that almost one in three of unemployed households in East Germany have less than 5 per cent of comparable average disposable household incomes. Even in West Germany, they have over 20 per cent of comparable incomes.[4]

☐ Children and young people are a particularly high-risk group in terms of relative poverty levels throughout the EC (50 per cent of comparable household income). They are on average twice as likely to face the threat of poverty as adult age groups. The grounds for this include the higher risk of unemployment for single parents and foreigners and inadequate social security benefit provision where both parents in families with several children lose their jobs.[5]

☐ Even when relative figures are compared over a specific period, i.e. since the beginning of the eighties, the unemployed have been the losers in the struggle over funding allocation. Disposable household income has only fallen in *real* terms for this type of household. Real income in all other types of households (self-employed, employees, pensioners, households on supplementary benefit) has risen by between 4 per cent and 30 per cent.[6]

Monitoring absolute figures over a given period puts things in perspective far more. Many of the victims manage to make their way out of the low income bracket again in the medium term.[7] On the other hand, panel studies have shown that the unemployed, in particular, experience long periods of poverty. In other words, whereas those in work only run a 1 per cent risk of falling below the so-called 50 per cent threshold of disposable household income, over 10 per cent of the unemployed are at risk.[8]

Social security and its shortcomings

The few figures available on poverty in low-income groups in Germany reveal great gaps in the social security system. Paradoxically, unemployment benefit can no longer fulfil its primary function when it is most needed for many of the victims. It is unable to guarantee a relative socio-cultural minimum level at times where there is a high risk of unemployment. The reasons for this can be found in the basic elements of the security system itself which was devised during a boom period and has proven to be relatively inflexible and very patchy in relation to eradicating poverty. However, these findings were discovered some time ago and the political methods introduced as a result may also be at fault (see below).

A secure income is provided under the German unemployment benefit system. It is designed to meet a number of targets which are no longer compatible with the current system, either in isolation or as a group, in the light of recent job market crises.

(i)   Unemployment benefit is intended to secure a basic income for those at risk and is meant to substitute supplementary benefit (minimum level of income provision).

(ii) Unemployment benefit is also intended to reflect a person's previous financial position in terms of the last rate of pay received to prevent loss of financial standing during periods of unemployment (function of securing financial position).

(iii) Unemployment is intended to be a less attractive status than the status of employment. Benefit payment is to be assigned a subsidiary role. Pressure is to be exerted to promote self-help ('less eligibility').

Minimum level of income provision

Unemployment benefit is not based on a minimum level even at the lower end of the scale. It is based on the last net income.

In real terms, losing your job means the loss of 50 per cent of your last net income, compensated for to some extent by slightly higher income-related government transfer payments for children and to cover housing costs. The system does not therefore provide a minimum level of income for those on low wages, or with a history of part-time work or high family-related costs (a single breadwinner, with several children and high housing costs). The result is that many unemployed people are also forced to apply for social security. The estimated figure is around 15 per cent.

A whole series of groups are excluded by the system from receiving benefit if they are unable to provide proof of specific minimum requirements in terms of hours of work. Young people who are unable to find work in jobs where national insurance is compulsory are discriminated against predominantly in this respect. There are also housewives who have not been in employment for some years and now want to return to work. Gaps in the social security system are revealed by comparing the number of people who are registered as unemployed with those receiving benefit. Over 20 per cent of those on the unemployment register do not receive benefit.

Benefit levels ultimately depend on age and length of previous employment (positive effect) or unemployment (negative effect) in their current form. In other words, comparatively old employees who have been in employment and paid compulsory national insurance for a number of years receive unemployment benefit at a level of over 50 per cent of their last net salary for a relatively long period. Yet others have to settle for lower benefit for shorter periods. This means that the following groups are faced with the threat of poverty under the current system:

- young people without any entitlement to unemployment benefit
- women who have taken time out to bring up a family
- those employed on a low wage and in low income groups
- part-time workers with relatively low take-home pay
- the long-term unemployed
- families with only one breadwinner and/or several children

Security of financial position with benefits

This objective has not been achieved either, because benefit payments are not normally high enough to provide a secure financial position. Long-term studies show that the unemployed are forced to use up their savings to a large extent and people in long-term unemployment are in acute danger of sliding into debt. This applies from the outset where benefit payments fall below the minimum level of income. The benefit system also contains certain *benefit cuts*, based on the following principle: the longer a person is unemployed, the lower the benefit payments.

These individual benefit cuts are contained in the following policy instruments:

(i) So-called 'unemployment benefit' provides a nominal level of 68 per cent or 63 per cent of net income and is payable for one year only. The maximum is two and a half years for older workers and longer periods of employment. This is followed by 'supplementary benefit' which is around 10 per cent below this nominal level and leads to a real loss in income of over 50 per cent compared to previous income from employment. The drop in income as a result of the changeover from unemployment benefit to supplementary benefit can be seen from average figures for benefit payments. Unemployed men in West Germany received on average 1,200 DM in unemployment benefit per month in 1991 and 920 DM in supplementary benefit. In East Germany, figures were well below this at 940 DM and 750 DM respectively. Unemployed women in West Germany receive on average 200 DM less than their male counterparts in both East and West Germany.

(ii) Benefit may be reassessed for long-term claims to determine whether the worker is still able to find a job in his trade to match his qualifications in the current job market. The longer the period of unemployment, the greater the risk of de-skilling. The German Employment Office may reduce a person's benefit if the chances of his/her finding a job are diminished.

Obligation to work

Benefit entitlement is always dependent on an obligation to work. Job offers must be accepted. There are exceptions which are based on the same principle as before: the longer the unemployment, the lower the status.

Job centres may exercise a wide range of sanctions if an unemployed person does not accept a job vacancy which is offered. Initially, unemployment benefit may be cut for a limited period. In cases of consistent 'refusal to accept work', that person may lose their entitlement to unemployment benefit altogether.

Pressure concerning the job market and self-help is mainly applied for bureaucratic reasons. German employment agencies are frequently overtaxed in their role as employment agencies and advice centres. They are also unsuitable in many ways due to their bureaucratic lines of communication. In addition, selective pressure is applied. Many jobs allocated by the German Employment Office are for short-term, low-paid work and are therefore only suitable for unskilled or semi-skilled workers. This, in turn, affects the poor again.

German social policy response

How has the original theory of unemployment benefit been affected by this highly volatile situation?

There now follows a brief description of how this system has been deployed as a policy instrument in official social policy. The aim is to find out what effect this has had on the objectives mentioned in the introduction, such as providing a minimum level of income, a secure financial position based on benefits, and promoting self-help.

Official economic and social policies are pursuing an inherently contradictory strategy at the expense of social security, which is based on the following elements:

On one hand, the government is misappropriating social security funds to cover the cost of reunification. A large proportion of income-related benefit payments made in East Germany (pensions, unemployment benefit) are being earned by workers in West Germany and used in the East on social transfer payments.

On the other hand, efforts are being made to cap social budget increases even in these times of crisis. In fact, social security costs overall are being cut in relative terms. Social security benefit (in terms of GDP) has fallen by 4 per cent since 1980 (1980: 33.7 per cent, 1992: 29.8 per cent).

A model of this kind cannot operate successfully in a recession. The consequences are:

- benefit cuts
- an increased tax burden with higher income tax and national insurance contributions

The effects on unemployment benefit are described below:

(i) The government presented a bill before parliament to amend the job promotion law (Arbeitsfrderungsgesetz). According to this, both unemployment benefit and supplementary benefit are to be cut by 2 per cent on average.
Supplementary benefit is to be limited to two years. The retraining allowance is also to be cut slightly. Subsidies for

short-time workers are to be stopped after six months. Bad-weather allowance is to be abolished altogether.

(ii) Unemployment contributions amounted to 4.2 per cent of gross income in 1985. In 1987 they were increased to 4.3 per cent and in 1991 they rose sharply to 6.8 per cent. The last increase in 1991 was originally intended to apply for a limited period and seems to be here to stay for the foreseeable future. There has been a good deal of budgetary reassignment between the various social security schemes in recent years to prevent any overall rise in gross staff costs. This has met with some degree of success, depending on the financial position of the respective social security scheme. One thing is clear though, and that is that this system is no longer operating effectively. Rising unemployment contributions in 1991 were offset at the time by cutting pension contributions. These will have to be revoked in 1994 again due to pension funding problems. This, in turn, accounts for the record levels of tax deductions in 1993/94. Income tax and employee contributions rose to a record level of 33.5 per cent of gross salary in 1993 (1980: 28.7 per cent) and accounted for over 35 per cent in 1994 to cover the increase in pension contributions.[9]

Unemployment benefit cuts are to be accompanied by social security rate capping. The future of the fine network of means-tested benefits providing a minimum level of income which was set up at such great expense is now the subject of political debate. To prevent the burden on social security from rising as a result of unemployment benefit cuts, standard rates are no longer to be linked to wages or prices. In other words, there will be no further increase in social security benefit before 1996.

Open questions on the challenges facing a social policy designed to combat poverty

Let us return to our original statement and the example of 'passive' labour market policy in Germany (to secure income in unemployment). This was intended to illustrate how far the social policy of 'social citizenship' had progressed so far, or how far we are away from it. A series of open questions and proposals based on this example are listed below. These need to be addressed by European social security systems providing a secure income and economic integration if the threat of poverty in times of mass unemployment is to be taken seriously. Problems affecting specific individual groups will not be discussed in depth. Basic design principles for social security systems will be analysed critically in relation to Germany.

Morals in the discussion on social policy

The national climate of debate may ultimately be the governing factor affecting this extremely sensitive and complex subject. In what spirit is the discussion on public funding allocations being conducted? The ruling parliamentary parties in the conservative/liberal camp in Germany are clearly deliberately inciting conflict within the debate. They are certainly not promoting or command-ing mainstream support in defence of minor issues, such as 'budget-ary consolidation' and 'locational protection', but cornering and crippling the debate as a result. In other words, the allocation debate is deliberately being driven against the 'takers' by the givers. This will adversely affect social security benefit.

The social democrats are unable to counter this pressure for fear of alienating their main body of voters and potential voters from the centre. They are tending to compromise more (damage limitation) without making a stand in defence of the weaker mem-bers of society in the allocation debate.

In times of stagnating social security and government expendi-ture rates, there is no voice to speak out in defence of the poor. They are clearly unable to defend their own position adequately in the political debate. The victims are unlikely to find support within the middle class coalition groups. And potential defenders of 'allocation on moral grounds', such as religious and union affili-ations or local authority groups, are being influenced by their supporters as well. The erosion of group affiliation is already wide-spread in every German metropolis, yet there is still no sign of any real long-term, independent group emerging to take their place.

Public intervention at subsistence level

One effect of this rather diffuse position has been uncertainty in the public debate, as to where poverty begins and when urgent action is required in social policy. German social security levels are revised annually in an obscure and complex process which has nevertheless increased in line with real income by and large over the past 15 years. Yet, some aspect of benefit is always being targeted and subjected to harsh, and often unwarranted, criticism by members of the government and others. Benefit for specific groups is then cut (pensions in 1993) or increased (single parents in 1993) accordingly. A proper scientific debate on moral codes is needed instead to provide a legitimate decision-making process, involving the state parliaments, if possible.

Relationship between income from employment and income from social security

Efforts to implement targets for the few funds available for income transfer payments has resulted in a counter-productive co-existence. As soon as people on unemployment benefit get a job, their income from social security is stopped. Low contributions are their only incentive. This arbitrary limit is counter-productive because it tends to punish independent initiative rather than reward it, and prevents a smooth and flexible transition from unemployment to employment. Obviously, unlimited benefit payments cannot be made for people with jobs. The negative effects on regular income from employment are tangible (incentive to accept low wages, relieving the burden on tariff partners to secure a basic living wage). No European nation would ever seriously consider providing a general basic social security which was not means-tested. This would be out of the question on account of the high financial burden involved. On the other hand, there does appear to be scope in Germany, at least, for tolerating the co-existence of income from social security and income from employment, instead of encouraging the many forms of black marketeering within the grey area of the economy, or inactivity as a result of strict demarcation.

Minimum level of income and benefits

It will be extremely difficult to define this proposed limit for income from employment and income from social security with this system of benefits. Contributions would require substantial mainstream support, as the funding received would only be paid out to high risk cases (causal relation). It would also be expected that benefit payments were based on the level of contributions paid in eligible cases (benefit principle). These two expectations would prevent these contributions from being used specifically to target poverty. Tax-funded systems, such as those in Scandinavia show that although these are certainly more flexible, they are based on a much broader social consensus (see above). In Germany we will have to consider whether our social security system could not be implemented more effectively with tax-funded transfers which provide a minimum level of income, where possible.

Incentives and controls

Positive incentives and negative controls on abuse are closely related. Contribution-based systems like those in Germany today with models providing *limited* support lead to a variety of intersection points with their definition of at-risk cases, or borderline cases, for which *this specific* benefit is not intended. The dual responsibility of a number of systems to provide similar living conditions and deal with the complex issue of eligibility, as a result, produces an atmosphere which tends to make the applicant feel controlled and compelled to justify his need. It is not the positive act of overcoming his difficult living conditions which then takes priority, but the sectoral demarcation of benefit entitlement. In Germany fear of potential abuse has taken hold both within social security and tax-funded benefit. The paying majority are always presented as the perfect example to the fortunate minority of social security recipients in an ideal world. Consequently it is hardly surprising that policy aimed at 'controlling abuse' can expect to receive wide approval. Yet, it is never quite clear exactly who or what is being 'abused' and what the actual legitimate purpose of unemployment benefit is.

Active and passive job market policy

The annual budget funding row over German unemployment benefit is symptomatic of this split in the debate. How much should be reserved for training, retraining and job creation? How much funding will be needed simply for income transfer payments? On an international scale, active job market policy funding varies substantially (as a percentage of GDP). Denmark, Sweden and Finland are the leaders with over 5 per cent. Japan, Switzerland and the US are at the bottom with 1 per cent. Germany is in the middle with 3.5 per cent and does not fare badly compared to France (2.7 per cent) and Britain (2.3 per cent).[10]

On the other hand, this budget item is also an indicator of how far EC states are prepared actively to accept responsibility for the professional reintegration of those at risk. German trends over the past 15 years have reflected every possible form of intervention and this clearly reveals the uncertainty among those in power. These trends include moderate intervention under the flagship of the Keynesian programme, radical cuts to government employment programmes, widescale intervention in the former GDR to aid transition, and budget cuts and new employment programs in 1994, the election year. Anything is possible!

Cash incentives, self-help and individual assistance

The main priority in government social policy must clearly be to guarantee a secure living wage for the unemployed. Yet, it is essential for their professional reintegration that victims of unemployment continue to feel personally motivated and challenged. Large-scale social security systems directed primarily at providing cash incentives are not flexible enough to respond to these individual needs. There is often a gulf between actual living conditions and the way these are assessed by standard benefit agencies.

Even standardisation of working conditions in terms of minimum wages, working hours and protective clauses in contracts of employment tend to widen the gulf between workers and jobless people in times of mass unemployment because the terms of employment are fixed and negotiation is largely superseded.

Deregulation in supply-oriented policy is no longer the answer. This could endanger the achievements of the European labour movement. They are now beginning to achieve a great deal in terms of basic living wages and humane working conditions. But a reassessment of those seeking work and job opportunities will be required, at best with a government-funded sector providing self-help and an informal economy.

The roots of the labour and union movements are based in the support of the movement for its impoverished members. These roots need to be revived. It is doubtful whether unions can be persuaded, as their interest representation is primarily in defence of the worker in employment. They are consequently understandably defensive about the subject of unemployment. Local authority action groups would appear to have a better chance. Governments must be made to realise that they have only done *half* of their job in providing for the unemployed and they must develop a second operational level to address current living conditions in conjunction with local employment agencies as part of government social policy.

Job creation within an 'active job market policy' can extend beyond the creation of regular government-funded jobs. This should also include systematic promotion of *community action* groups and *self-help* organisations. Reallocation of income from employment and social security (see above) may help, as may government or externally-funded local authority self-help organis-ations.

The *subjective* effects of long-term exclusion from the world of work must ultimately be taken seriously as potential obstacles to integration. Cash incentive policy instruments tend to fail in most cases in this respect. In many instances, the long-term unem-ployed and young people who have never had a job need a bridge in the form of *individual assistance* and protected working con-ditions. The longer mass unemployment continues throughout Europe, the greater the risk that unemployment itself will become a mass hindrance to integration. Financial provision often silences the victims but it can never activate or motivate them.

Conclusion

One priority in the policy of 'social citizenship' is to examine individual elements within the social security system critically to obtain feedback on whether it is helping to eradicate poverty, for example. Unemployment benefit plays a crucial role in this. As with all amendments to development projects, we must not forget that this innovation can only succeed if it is introduced into a climate where the principle of shared responsibility is accepted. Policies aimed at eradicating poverty can only motivate in the long term as part of a liberal concept of shared individual responsibility. Securing a basic living wage in the broadest sense can only encour-age individual self-determination within the context of 'social citi-zenship'.

6 A NEW SOCIAL POLICY FOR THE 'ACTIVE SOCIETY'

Chris Pond

In his presentation to a recent European Commission conference on Employment in Europe,[1] then President Delors spoke of the need for Europe to meet the challenges of the next century by becoming an 'active society'. His purpose was not simply to respond to accusations that the European Union had become gripped by a form of economic and social 'sclerosis' but also to promote a positive vision of society based on participation and partnership, citizenship and cohesion.

The recent 'Green Paper' on European Social Policy published by the Commission clarifies the concept. An 'active' society, it explains, is one in which:

> there is a wider distribution of income, achieved by means
> other than simple social security transfers, and in which each
> individual feels able to contribute not only to production (as
> part of the search for full employment) but also via a more
> active participation in the development of society as a whole.
> An 'active' society is also one which has the ability to provide
> an adequate supply of 'collective goods' – such as education,
> health and social protection systems – which are required to
> ensure its innovative capacities and its ability to adjust quickly.[2]

In this paper, we argue that there is a need for a new European Social Policy to meet the challenge of increasing poverty, inequality and fragmentation within the European Union. The economic difficulties facing the Union have led some to argue that social protection and labour market regulation must be sacrificed in the attempt to restore economic prosperity. There is an inevitable trade-off, they contend, between economic progress and social justice.

Although this view, promoted enthusiastically by the UK government, has some support elsewhere in the Union, it conflicts

110

with the traditional European model of development, in which social progress is seen as a prerequisite of economic prosperity, not as its alternative. Attempting to strip the social dimension out of European development would result in wider social divisions and slower economic growth.

A policy to meet the challenges of the next century must build on the partnership between economic and social progress, but must also move away from the model of a passive welfare state encouraging dependency and militating against social cohesion. The welfare state should promote citizenship and participation, not dependency and subjection. Moreover, a new social policy must be so integrated with economic policy that it seeks to tackle the underlying causes of poverty and inequality, rather than simply alleviating the symptoms.

The challenge of European poverty

Recent estimates by the European Commission suggest that more than 50 million people – approximately 15 per cent of the population – now live in poverty.[3] Many of these are excluded from full participation in society.

Such exclusion is not simply a matter of lack of employment, although this is a major factor. Even for those in employment, exclusion can result from an income which is inadequate to allow those affected to participate fully in society as citizens, and to enjoy the rights and responsibilities common in mature democracies.

Nor is poverty itself the determining factor. One quarter of those defined as poor throughout the EC 12 are UK citizens. Some of these might have an income higher, in absolute terms, than that enjoyed elsewhere in the Community. Yet the scale of inequality in Britain diminishes the relative position of the UK poor, depriving them of the ability to participate fully as citizens in the society in which they live. Political democracy is stifled if economic democracy, a fair and equal sharing of the nation's resources, is absent.

Having stabilised during the 1980s throughout most of the Community, poverty and exclusion are now on the increase, partly because of the cyclical effects of the recession and partly for structural reasons. In some Member States, policy choices have further exacerbated the problem.

What went wrong?

It appears that the European welfare state, which for so many years seemed to deliver security and prosperity, is now failing to provide adequate protection. Certainly, pressures on social expenditure have increased due to rising unemployment, demographic change and political preferences. The burden of financing the welfare state is beginning to be perceived as intolerable.

Although the problems are acute, they are not necessarily new. Even before the present economic crisis, and almost half a century after the establishment of the modern welfare state, problems of poverty and inequality persisted. Why?

The answer is probably to be found in the initial premise on which the European welfare state was based: that, except at the macro-economic level of demand management, interventions in the forces that generate poverty and inequality were not the legitimate role of government. Such intervention would result in a misallocation of resources and a lower level of economic efficiency.

However, fiscal measures to alleviate the worst effects of this process 'after the event' were considered appropriate. A social security system could provide a 'safety net', financed by progressive taxation, designed not only to finance social expenditure but to trim the worst excesses of wealth and incomes as well. A health system and an education service would ensure a minimum standard of provision, available regardless of income. Describing the origins of the modern European socio-economic system, the Commission's Green Paper explains:

> Social policy was largely based on the transfer of income to
> the needy through the tax system, and the development of
> social security systems based in certain countries on
> contributions by employers and workers so as to maintain
> incomes in times of need.

The system was highly successful, during the prosperous decades following the War, in ensuring the maintenance of minimum standards. The welfare state acted as a form of 'savings bank', into which people paid during periods of their life-cycle when their incomes exceeded their needs, and from which they drew during periods when their needs exceeded their incomes. However, the system was never designed to tackle the root causes of poverty and, when the good times came to an end, the underlying inequalities reasserted themselves. Poverty (one of the giants which Beveridge planned to slay) had reawoken. The health service (certainly in Britain) served to raise general standards of health, yet social class differences in mortality and morbidity persisted.[4] Educational standards were improved but the greatest beneficiaries of education expenditure were the already well-to-do. Meanwhile, higher income groups were easily able to circumnavigate the effects of nominally progressive tax systems.

The welfare state that began as a democratic institution came to be perceived, by those who used it most, as unaccountable and inaccessible. The pressures on public finances and the increasing expenditure required to maintain social welfare have led some governments to tighten the rules on eligibility and to introduce greater selectivity in the provision of benefits.

The fabric of the social safety net has been damaged, and the stigma and indignity imposed on claimants has increased. The universality of welfare provision, intended to improve independence, has given way to an increasing selectivity which consigns people to dependency. In some countries, social welfare has become an instrument of exclusion, not a means of reducing it.[5]

To some extent this was inevitable. Depending so heavily on fiscal transfers, the welfare state was vulnerable to downturns in the economic cycles and to shifts in political ideology.

There seems little prospect that social expenditure will be increased to meet the growing problems of poverty, even in those Member States more committed to welfare provision. Moreover, there is a general lack of confidence in the ability of macro-economic demand management to alleviate the problems through increasing output and incomes, even were this allowed by the Maastricht monetary conditions. It seems that poverty, exclusion and social division will inevitably increase, unless an alternative strategy can be identified.

Social Europe or deregulation

Despite the difficulties now facing the European Union, the member governments have committed themselves to certain objectives through the Maastricht Treaty, including:

- a high level of employment and social protection;
- the raising of the standard of living and the quality of life;
- economic and social cohesion and solidarity between all the Member States.

These objectives are at the centre of the current debate within Europe about the way forward. The UK government argues explicitly that a high level of social protection conflicts with employment creation. It argues that Europe's citizens must accept a lower standard of living in order to be competitive with the rest of the world.

Economic and social cohesion within the UK have been damaged by recent policy choices: the real incomes of the poorest declined by 14 per cent during the 1980s, while those of the richest increased by over 60 per cent.[6]

The other partners of the Union consider that Britain is seeking to compete, not only with the rest of the world but with other Member States, through a policy of social devaluation, reducing the living standards of its own citizens to gain a competitive advantage. Indeed, the Department of Trade and Industry has been advertising in the newspapers of other Member States, encouraging firms to take advantage of Britain's low wages by investing in the UK.[7]

UK ministers proudly claim that this approach is gaining ground, and that the Commission's draft White Paper on Employment, Competitiveness and Growth has been amended to remove references to be employment protection and the social dimension.

Yet the UK approach remains fundamentally in conflict with the European model, as reiterated in the Commission's Green Paper on Social Policy.

> It is important to underline that high standards of social protection have been a major contributory factor in Europe's economic success in the past. Many would argue that high social standards should not be seen as an optional extra, or a luxury which can be done without once times get hard, but rather as an integral part of a competitive economic model. The debate between this view and those who argue that Europe's present level of social standards have become unaffordable goes to the heart of the issue.[8]

Social protection and economic success

The Commission's argument that social progress is a prerequisite for economic success has a long tradition, even within the UK itself. Winston Churchill argued as long ago as 1909 that 'decent conditions make for industrial efficiency and increase rather than decrease competitive power'.[9] The minimum wage which he established at that time was abolished in August 1993, leaving Britain as the only country in Europe without legal pay protection for the poorest.

Harold Macmillan (later Lord Stockton) was leader of the Conservative Party in 1946 when he welcomed the passing of a Fair Wages provision for Britain as 'the protector, certainly of the standard of living of the workers, but also of the standards of competence and honour of industry as a whole'.[10] Attempts by the Commission to introduce measures to ensure an 'equitable wage' have been resisted by the UK government, which abolished its own Fair Wages Resolution in 1981.

The assertion that social policy has a fundamental role to play in achieving economic success is not, therefore, new. It is firmly based on sound economic principles:

(i)   Inequality is not only socially divisive but economically wasteful. It prevents many citizens from fulfilling their potential or making a full contribution;

(ii) Inequality deprives economies of effective spending power by shifting resources from those whose spending propensity is highest to those whose saving and import propensity is highest;

(iii) Short-term competition based on cost-cutting undermines investment in training or better techniques of production, damaging productivity, raising unit labour costs and reducing competitiveness;

(iv) Social expenditure is also a form of social investment, enhancing the stock of human capital and creating a climate of stability;

(v)   Partnership and solidarity improve productivity by reducing conflict and tensions within industry and the wider economy;

(vi) Uncertainty is the enemy of flexibility. Without protection of their employment and living standards people are less willing to take risks and accept change.

Evidence to support these principles is abundant. Japan and Germany have been the two most prominent examples of economic success, based on social partnership and a relatively equal distribution of incomes. The UK and the United States, by contrast, have suffered from their extreme and increasing inequalities.

The Anglo-American experiment

Britain is a low-wage economy within Europe. Even before abolition of its minimum wage system, Britain had a higher proportion of its workforce earning less than the Council of Europe 'decency threshold' than any other Member State. The recent *Employment in Europe* report, published by the European Commission points out that the UK's national income only compares with that of other Member States because of a much higher participation rate and longer working hours for full-time males:

> Average labour costs in manufacturing in the highest UK region, the South East, were still some 35 per cent below the average level in Germany in 1988 and around 15 per cent below the level in Northern Italy or France, outside Paris. This means that the level was similar to that in the South of Italy. Labour costs in most other parts of the UK were therefore significantly lower than in the Southern Italian regions – in Northern Ireland, some 30 per cent lower.[11]

Despite this low level of wages, Britain is relatively uncompetitive. This is because productivity is low, pushing unit labour costs in the UK to a level very much higher than the EC average. In part, this low level of productivity is a result of the fact that Britain, being the only Member State without limits to working time, has the longest working hours (for men) in the EC. Staff turnover and absenteeism are high by European standards, and training is poor.

These factors are directly related to the low wages themselves: the undervaluation of any factor of production will lead to misallocation of resources. Employers have no incentive to invest in training if labour is cheap and readily available. Indeed, any firm that attempts to pursue a high training/high investment strategy risks being undercut by others seeking short-term competitive advantage by cost-cutting. In the absence of regulation, only those firms with control over their product market can afford to undertake such investment.

The United States has been held up as an example of the success of the deregulation strategy. Even those committed to the European model are haunted by the fact that the USA has created more jobs during the 1980s than Europe. Yet there is no mystery as to how this happened: the United States saw virtually no productivity growth during the last decade, so that each percentage point of economic growth generated more employment than was the case in Europe. The jobs created were poorly paid, insecure and unstable. They did not represent sustainable employment creation.

Robert Reich, US Secretary of Labour, informed the European Commission Conference on Employment in Europe during October 1993 that the USA faced two jobs crises: the first was the quality of jobs; the second the quantity. The American people's traditional confidence in progress, he explained, had been damaged by the experience of the 1980s, making them less willing to accept change, to take risks or to exhibit the flexibility that modern economies require.

Although the UK is the most enthusiastic advocate of the deregulation strategy, its own experience is the best example of the failure of such a strategy. Britain is not only a low-wage but also a deregulated economy. Employment protection is now probably the weakest in Europe, with little provision in the form of maternity rights, protection against unfair dismissal, equality at work, protection for children and young people or minimum wages. Expenditure on social protection is lower, as a proportion of GDP, than in most other EC Member States.

Yet the male unemployment rate, even taking account of statistical manipulation, is amongst the highest in the Union, albeit disguised by a high female part-time participation rate. Deregulation has not allowed Britain to create employment, and it has certainly not delivered prosperity. Indeed, it has left the British economy in a fragile and unstable condition which has reduced its ability to recover from recession.

A new policy for the next century

The British and American experiments encourage little confidence that deregulation and a reduction in social protection offer a solution to Europe's malaise. As well as damaging economic prospects, such policies damage the fabric of society itself.

Moreover, such policies encourage dependency and passivity, discouraging the flexibility and willingness to change that is so essential for a dynamic economy. Jaques Delors' vision of an active society requires the full participation of people as citizens, contributing fully to economic progress.

A simple increase in spending on social protection would not necessarily solve the problems of poverty and inequality that Europe faces. The vulnerability of a fiscally-based European welfare state is clear. Nor would an expansion of social protection achieve the objective of building an active society. As Mr Troels Anderson, the Chair of the Social Affairs Committee of the Council of European Municipalities and Regions has argued: 'To rely on revenue transfers risks threatening people's dignity, self-respect and sense of responsibility'.[12]

The European Social Charter has been criticised for its emphasis on the rights of employees, focusing on the active rather than on the inactive population.[13] Yet this emphasis provides a basis on which to build a future social policy which is compatible with the objective of economic progress.

Instead of a fiscally-based welfare state, the new challenge is to tackle the root causes of poverty and inequality, not just the symptoms. Instead of viewing social policy as an optional extra, it should be seen as an integral part of economic policy. And economic policy priorities should be chosen to ensure the attainment of the Treaty objectives: economic and social cohesion; a high level of employment and social protection; raising the standard and quality of life. How is this to be achieved?

The definition of social policy needs to be expanded beyond social protection, to include a structure of rights and responsibilities for European citizens:

Employment generation

Unemployment is wasteful and expensive, both to the individual and to society. A European programme of economic recovery, with the creation of high quality employment as its primary objective would reduce the fiscal burden on the state, increase output, improve living standards and cohesion.

Employment rights

Employment protection, minimum wage provisions, equality at work, limits to working hours, the protection of children and young people at work, maternity and paternity rights would all enhance productivity and flexibility.

Training and investment in human capital

This is not a solution to poverty and unemployment, since the main causes of these are not lack of skills. But training would enhance productivity overall and increase the dignity and independence of citizens.

Childcare provision

This should be seen as an economic as much as a social policy. The absence of childcare provision prevents people making their full contribution to economic activity. Childcare allows parents to compete in the labour market, if they so wish, on equal terms.

Social protection

The measures above would reduce dependency on welfare. We need to reassert the role of social security as a right of all citizens at times when they need it – a system into which all contribute and from which all have a right to draw. Selectivity not only reduces the adequacy of social protection, it also increases dependency and stigma.

The list of ingredients for a new social policy cannot be exhaustive. The purpose is not to provide a blue-print for a policy appropriate to meet the challenges of the next century but to establish the principles on which that policy should be based. Europe should argue the case for equality between economic and social policy with confidence, as the best way of ensuring prosperity and social cohesion. The alternatives are bleak.

7 NEW POLICIES FOR THE TWENTY-FIRST CENTURY: A COMMON EC APPROACH

Bernd Schulte

European community social security law

The activities of the European Community in the field of social security can be divided into two quite distinct categories, namely:

□   the activities carried out in pursuance of EC social policy in order to bring about an improvement in the social security systems of the Member States, and

□   the intervention of the Community institutions in operating the social security laws of the Member States for the purpose of ensuring the free movement of workers.

The realisation of the first objective – that of improving the social security systems of the Member States – has been attempted without great success by means of *harmonisation*; and has been replaced since the beginnings of the 1990s by a strategy aiming at the *convergence* of national social policies. The second objective – ensuring the free movement of workers – is achieved by means of *co-ordination*.

The harmonisation of social security in EC Member States

When the Treaty of Rome was being negotiated in the 1950s, France argued for the inclusion of provisions for social harmonisation. But the other negotiators of the Treaty, especially the Federal Republic of Germany, did not accept France's proposal that the harmonisation of social security was necessary to achieve the objectives of the Common Market, such as free enterprise. The Treaty does not, therefore, contain any specific proposals for harmonisation; it contains several provisions which can be used as a basis for harmonisation, but which have been used only very reluctantly in this respect up to now.[1]

Article 100 of the EEC Treaty provides for the approximation of laws where such laws 'directly affect the establishment of the functioning of the Common Market'. This provision can be used as a legal basis for Community action in the sphere of social security, provided it can be established that it is necessary for the proper functioning of the Common Market to have uniformity in certain areas of the social security laws of the Member States. Article 117 of the EEC Treaty says that Member States agree upon the need to promote improved working conditions and improved standards of living for workers. It states that this will ensue from the procedures provided in the Treaty and from the functioning of the Common Market which will 'favour the harmonisation of the social systems'. It does not give the Community institutions any power to harmonise, assuming instead that harmonisation will be the natural consequence of the economic union. Article 118 of the EEC Treaty imposes upon the Commission the duty of providing a close collaboration with Member States in certain matters of social policy, one of which is social security. The competence to take decisions under Article 118 of the EEC Treaty lies, however, with national governments (and continues to do so after enactment of the Single European Act).

In addition, harmonisation has been advocated as the sole means of achieving *integration* in the economic, social and political sense. This raises the question of whether the Member States actually want such total integration; and it seems rather doubtful that they do. Harmonisation in all spheres of Community activity was greatly resented in the late 1960s and early 1970s because Member States disliked large-scale interference with their legal systems, their systems of social protection, and hence their life styles. Even if one accepts that Member States really desire total integration, it is by no means certain that the harmonisation of social security is necessary to achieve it. Finally, it has been argued that harmonisation of social security leads to a lowering of social security standards. This seems, however, not to be true. When harmonisation first takes place, the highest standards within the EC may be taken as the norm on the assumption that no State will suffer a lowering of its standards. Besides, when a certain area of social security is harmonised this does not necessarily mean that Member States cannot subsequently introduce improvements. For example minimum standards may well be improved by Member States provided such improvements do not run contrary to Community policy (see the new Article 118a of the EEC Treaty referring to improvements in the 'working environment', i.e., in safety at work).[2]

The convergence of social security objectives within the Community

In 1986 the Commission transmitted a Communication to the Council entitled 'Problems of Social Security – Areas of Common Interest' which identified a certain number of problem areas of common interest to the Twelve Member States: (i) financing problems; (ii) demographic problems, and (iii) marginalisation.

(i) *financing problems*: social security schemes have been under pressure from the increase in public expenditure on social protection. This is a result of persistent high-level unemployment and changing demographic structures, which are increasing the pressure on the old-age and sickness insurance sectors, while at the same time the flow of incoming revenue is slowing down.

(ii) *demographic problems*: fertility has been declining in all Member States since the mid-1960s with a resulting decline in the working population, which will lead to a heavier burden on the economy, especially in terms of social charges.

(iii) *marginalisation*: i.e., the problem of the 'new poor'. The existing social protection schemes – mainly the social security and social assistance schemes – do not cover the whole population, but often exclude young unemployed persons and restrict the duration or level of entitlement for other categories of the unemployed, especially the long-term unemployed. In addition to employment problems, new poverty is also caused by the increasing instability of the family situation, i.e., the growing number of divorces, separations and cases of cohabitation, which leave numerous persons without any individual rights to social benefits, as well as without rights derived from a spouse.

On the basis of an analysis of these problem areas the Commission proposed a range of actions and raised the question of whether it would be appropriate for Member States to discuss at Community level the objectives to be fixed for social protection schemes beyond the 1990s. The purpose of such an initiative would be to obviate the danger that Member States, within the framework of the completion of the Internal Market, might introduce social measures which would give them a competitive edge against other member countries, i.e., to prevent 'social dumping'. In addition, the quest for the convergence of long-term objectives would also overcome at least part of the opposition to the idea of gradually bringing into line existing social protection schemes within the Community.

At the Council on Social Affairs on 29 September 1989, consensus was achieved on the principle of the convergence of social protection objectives and policies in Europe. The Commission Action Programme on the Implementation of the 'Community Charter of Basic Social Rights for Workers' which was adopted by the European Council in Strasbourg on 8/9 December 1989 provides for the preparation of a Community recommendation on the subject.[3]

The Programme Relating to the Implementation of the Community Charter of Basic Social Rights for Workers[4] confirms first of all that because of the great variations in nature from one Member State of the Community to another, which reflect the history, traditions and social and cultural practices characteristic of each Member State and which cannot be called into question, there can be *no question of harmonising* the systems of social protection existing in these fields. The fact remains, however, that it would be worthwhile conducting in-depth deliberations on a strategy for achieving convergence on the objectives pursued by the various governments so as to determine how and under what conditions differences in the systems can be prevented from hindering free movement of workers. The Commission proposes to do this by means of a '*Recommendation on Social Protection: Convergence of Objectives*'.[5] The definition of *fundamental objectives* which are common to all Member States may lead to convergence in terms of the specific standards for each objective. This does not mean that legislative provisions have to be identical (as in a harmonisation strategy), but that the *effects* of national legislation implementing these objectives should be convergent. Such an approach does not necessarily imply changes in legislation; it might encompass, for example, methods judged to be particularly appropriate for solving specific problems (e.g. the solutions to the crucial problem of nursing care for the very old).

It is also considered important that progress towards the strategic objectives adopted should be assessed regularly at Community level, as convergence should be directed towards social progress and any deterioration in those Member States where standards are highest should, therefore, be avoided. In any case, convergence should be *flexible*, i.e., Member States should have enough freedom in the way in which they adapt their system. The Commission should support and encourage this convergence by studies, analysis, seminars and assessments. A further means of support could be the definition, at Community level, for certain principles and objectives which could be based, for example, on certain elements of the existing conventions of the International Labour Organisation and the Council of Europe. Such an approach would fit well into the picture shown at the beginning of the origins of supranational (EC) social security law.

The co-ordination of social security systems within the Community

Most European Community social security legislation is concerned with the protection of the social security rights of migrant workers moving within the Community, as the free movement of workers has always been one of the primary aims first of the European Coal and Steel Community and then of the European Economic Community. It is impossible to achieve this aim without the protection of the social security rights of the persons concerned. Workers will be reluctant to move from one Member State to another if they risk losing all the social security rights which they have gained throughout their previous working lives.

Article 51 of the Treaty of Rome, establishing the European Economic Community, goes further. It specifies what must be done at Community level to ensure that workers are not disadvantaged, or even penalised, in the exercise of their right of free movement which is one of the 'four freedoms' of the EEC Treaty (freedom of capital, freedom of goods, freedom of services, freedom of movement for workers) – to provide freedom of movement for workers; to this end, it makes arrangements to secure for migrant workers and their dependants:

(i) aggregation, for the purpose of acquiring and retaining the right to benefit of calculating the amount of benefits, of all periods taken into account under the laws of individual countries;

(ii) payment of benefits to persons resident in the territories of Member States.

These legal instruments do not envisage the creation of some sort of supranational social security system common to all Member States. But they co-ordinate the various social security systems of the Member States to enable them to interact in order to provide constant social protection for migrant workers who move from one Member State to another, as well as for the members of their family. Co-ordination does not alter the substance of the legal systems which are linked together except in so far as the scope of the national systems is widened. The social security rights of migrant workers are personalised in so far as they remain attached to them wherever they move in the Community. Article 51 of the EEC Treaty and the EEC Regulations Nos. 1408/71 and 574/72 implementing this provision are based on the fundamental principle of non-discrimination (Article 6 EC Treaty). This means that in social security matters there must be no difference in the treatment of nationals and non-nationals from other Member States. Equality of treatment of nationals and non-national migrant workers is attained by ensuring that the migrant workers' social security obligations as well as the rights arising out of these obligations are the same as those of the non-migrant workers. The migrant workers' contributions must, therefore, be calculated in the same manner as those of national workers.

European social policy has some of its most important origins in these social security provisions for *migrant workers* moving between Member States, which for a long time constituted and, perhaps, still do constitute, the 'social core' of the Community.[6] In reality these provisions have been an annex to EC policies to promote the freedom of movement of workers, as freedom of movement is seen as essential in order to forge the territories of the 12 Member States into a Single Market.

Since the objective of the Treaty of Rome was to construct a European Economic Community, little importance was attached to a common social policy as such. Social policy has always been the 'Cinderella' of EC policies.[7] However, a further important step towards the development of explicit social policy was taken in the 1970s, by the European Court of Justice, which gave practical meaning to the guarantee of *equal treatment for men and women* in labour law and social security laid down in Article 119 of the EEC Treaty ('equal pay for equal work'), and by a variety of legal instruments enacted by the Council. Since the mid-1970s the EC Council of Ministers has passed five directives referring to this objective.[8]

European social policy and the poor

Another important development in EC social policy was the recognition of the need to *combat poverty* as one of the European Community's priority areas of work. This evolved during the mid-1970s, with debates within Member States about the persistence of poverty which had emerged as a result of changes in family structure and rising unemployment.

The EC Commission set up three poverty programmes – 1975–80, 1984–8, 1989–94. These programmes aimed to stimulate political debate on poverty and social exclusion in the Member States, to permit the exchange of experience and the emergence of a series of networks of experts, practitioners and policymakers and to co-ordinate activities in the Member States for combating poverty and social exclusion. 'Poverty 3', which was approved following a Resolution of the European Council of the Heads of State and Governments of the 12 Member States in 1989, had a multi-dimensional approach to poverty. It was based on three key principles: 'multidimensionality of activities', 'partnership' and 'participation of the population'[9] and involved 27 model projects and 12 innovative initiatives in Europe. However, the five-year budget of 55 million ECUs (albeit more than twice the budget of the previous programme) worked out at less than one ECU for each poor person in the Community. 'Poverty 4' has been proposed by the European Commission but has not yet been approved by the Council.

Within the EC poverty programmes, the poor have been defined as:

> persons whose resources (material, cultural and social) are so limited as to exclude them from the minimum acceptable way of life in the Member State in which they live.[10]

This reflects the relative conception of poverty which emerged in the 1950s and 1960s. Poverty was to be considered relative to the resources and general standard of living of a particular society at a particular time. Poverty is seen not just as a shortage of money, but refers to situations of shortages or deprivation of various non-monetary characteristics such as education, vocational training, work capacity, health, housing, as well as leading to marginalis-ation and isolation.[11] According to this definition, poverty is the extreme form of inequality in living standards. Though insufficient income is only one aspect of poverty, it is, in general, the common denominator of all poverty situations and can therefore be a useful indicator of the extent of poverty. In the mid-1980s the proportion of persons with per capita disposable incomes below 50 per cent of the national average was

- particularly high (18 to 32 per cent) in Greece, Ireland, Portugal, Spain and the United Kingdom
- about average (15 per cent) in France and Italy
- relatively low (6 to 11 per cent) in Belgium, Denmark, Germany and the Netherlands[12]

Using the same definition, the Interim Report on the second Euro-pean Poverty Programme[13] estimated that the number of poor in the 12 Member States had increased from 38 million in 1975 to 44 million in 1985. Newer estimates from the European Commission which derive from household surveys increase the number of per-sons with low income in 1985 from 44 million to 50 million, corresponding to 15.4 per cent of the total population of the 12 Member States.[14]

Whereas the absolute level of poverty stabilised between 1975 and 1985, it changed in composition. Poverty among the elderly decreased at a time when their numbers increased as a proportion of the total population. Instead, poverty began increasingly to afflict the working age population and, especially, families with dependent children. This was linked to the rise in unemployment and the change in family structures, particularly the growing number of lone-parent families. The European Commission has warned that, at least in the short term, the creation of the Single European Market will bring significant social and economic dislo-cations which will have negative effects on certain areas and certain categories of people. These effects will add to the already large inequalities which exist between and within Member States of the Communities. Therefore, an increase in social exclusion and marginalisation is probable. Faced with this prospect, the European

Commission will have to tackle difficult questions concerning social protection, social exclusion, social cohesion and social citizenship which are issues of current political debate at the national as well as the EC level.[15]

The guarantee of minimum resources within the community

The Community Charter of Fundamental Social Rights of Workers

Though it is not valid for the Community as a whole, because the United Kingdom did not sign it, the Charter is highly important for the promotion of activities in the social field, both at the level of the Community and that of Member States, and it is important with respect to anti-poverty policy too.

The Charter, which constitutes a proclamation of fundamental rights, states that:

> according to the arrangements applying in each country . . . persons who have been unable either to enter or re-enter the labour market and have no means of subsistence must be able to receive sufficient resources and social assistance in keeping with their particular situation.

And that:

> according to the arrangements applying in each country . . . any person who has reached retirement age but who is not entitled to a pension or who does not have other means of subsistence, must be entitled to sufficient resources and to medical and social assistance specifically suited to his needs.

It remains the responsibility of the Member States to guarantee the rights proclaimed in the Charter. The Charter refers, however, to an Action Programme Relating to the Implementation of the Community Charter of the Fundamental Social Rights of Workers[16] which features a set of different elements. The Community's strategy with respect to social protection is intended to be flexible, progressive and based on a voluntary approach on the part of the Member States. It implies the definition of common objectives at

Community level relating to the convergence of social protection policies.[17]

Integration of the least privileged

In general, all European states which are Member States of the European Economic Space which came into being on 1 January 1994 (i.e., the twelve Member States of the European Union plus Austria, Finland, Iceland, Norway and Sweden), provide their citizens with almost universal coverage for the main functions of social protection: health, old age, maternity/family, employment and others. The importance of their systems of social protection is one of the most striking characteristics of these states, and the weight of their systems of social protection in economic and political terms, as well as their relevance for the living conditions of the citizens is much greater than, for instance, in the USA, Japan or in most other parts of the world.

The social protection systems of the Member States[18] are, however, not always in accord with the multidimensional, relative concept of poverty that underlies the Community programmes (see p. 128). Indeed, they are necessarily the products of different political and social concepts and need to be understood in a wider social policy context.

All EC Member States provide varying degrees of protection against the principal social risks of illness, maternity, invalidity, occupational accident and disease, old age, death with surviving dependants, unemployment and costs of children. This is mainly achieved through social security systems which postulate that every adult (male) should have the possibility, as well as the obligation, to earn continuing subsistence for himself and his immediate family through employment.

Expenditure on social protection as a percentage of GDP averages about 25 per cent, ranging in 1991 from about 20 per cent in Greece to more than 32 per cent in the Netherlands.[19]

Social security providing social protection against the above-mentioned contingencies is still today the main pillar of these systems of social protection, which differ traditionally from social assistance through the level of benefits provided and through the existence of fixed legal claims to benefits.

In recent years the legal character of social assistance benefits has been strengthened too, discretionary elements having been reduced and individual legal entitlements being formulated in terms of 'subjective rights'.

Against this background, social assistance schemes have moved away from the traditional Poor Law approach towards schemes which guarantee minimum resources and which aim at providing financial support to those members of society who do not have sufficient resources on their own or as members of the household in which they live (especially as members of the family to which they belong) by comparison with nationally established standards. This financial assistance aims at enabling the beneficiaries to have resources of an amount at least equal to that fixed by these standards.

However, guaranteed minimum income schemes and social assistance schemes which are primarily intended to relieve poverty and to support a minimum level of subsistence exist in only eight of the twelve EC Member States: Belgium, Denmark, France, Germany, Ireland, Luxembourg, Netherlands and the United Kingdom.[20] In these countries there is an individual right to a guaranteed minimum income: Belgium – minimum of subsistence (Minimum de moyens d'existence – minimex); Denmark – Social Bijstand; Germany – Sozialhilfe, i.e., Hilfe zum Lebensunterhalt; France – revenu minimum d'insertion (RMI) and aide social; Ireland – Supplementary Welfare Allowance (SWA); Luxembourg – revenu minimum garanti (RMG); Netherlands – Sociaal Bijstand; United Kingdom – Income Support and Family Credit. These schemes are mostly *general* minimum income schemes, i.e., they are available, on principle, to the whole population or at least to large categories of the population, even if in practice entitlement to benefits is subject to various conditions, in particular, conditions of age, nationality, length of residence, etc.

Furthermore, all these general minimum income schemes are means-tested. There is no scheme in any of these states which is based on the idea of a guaranteed basic income where a specified amount of money is given to any citizen irrespective of any further condition besides citizenship or residence in the particular Member State. Contrary to the concept of a guaranteed basic income, the existing minimum income arrangements in these states consist in the payment of a differential allowance to top up the resources already available to a household by a fixed amount.

In addition to this differential allowance the claimant (or the household) may also qualify for various supplementary allowances, in particular for assistance with the cost of accommodation or for special allowances (e.g. in the case of sickness, maternity, disability, or old age.

Whereas most Member States have fixed guaranteed amounts applicable throughout their territory, there are also regional variations in these amounts in some countries. The arrangements for assessing resources from which the differential allowance paid is calculated vary from one Member State to another, too. Often certain resources are excluded from this assessment (e.g. part of income from paid activity in order to create an incentive for work).

These guaranteed minimum income schemes or social assistance schemes are more or less similar in the following elements

(i)   they are based on the 'social assistance approach' which is distinguished from other forms of social provision by its subsidiary character and its emphasis on providing benefits only to those who prove need;

(ii)   their benefits are provided as of right;

(iii)   they are mostly universal, i.e., available in principle to all citizens (e.g. Germany, Netherlands), but partly specific, i.e., targeted to a specific segment of the population provided only in specific contingencies (e.g. France);

(iv)   as a rule they are meant to cover standard needs, but are in some cases designed to meet specific needs too;

(v)   in combination with other allowances, they sometimes also cover exceptional needs or supplementary expenses;

(vi)   benefits are, on principle, available for unlimited periods to those who are in need and who fulfil the qualifying conditions;

(vii)   they are means tested, mostly with a household or family as the assessment unit;

(viii) benefits are subsidiary to the claimant's income, capital and assets (with certain exceptions);

(ix)   they are, as a rule, financed by general taxation;

(x)   benefits are not reimbursable (with certain exceptions);

(xi)   they are, more or less, conditional on availability for work (certain categories of people are, however, exempt from this work condition e.g. the elderly, sick persons, disabled persons, persons with family obligations);

(xii) in some countries, eligibility is conditional on the availability
of reintegration measures into the labour market or in
society as a whole (e.g. France), whereas in other countries,
benefits which are to provide the social minimum are
concomitant with such measures (e.g. Germany);

(xiii) they are, to a varying degree, supplemented by private
charity and, at least partly, integrated into the voluntary
sector (e.g. Germany).[21]

The old discretionary public assistance has thus in most of these
countries been converted into a *right to assistance*, which includes
at least a right to financial assistance at a minimum level for
subsistence and for some degree of participation in the life of the
community.

At the same time, the old distinction between 'social assistance'
and 'social security' has been fading away, and social assistance is
considered more and more as one of the techniques by which the
welfare state provides income security for all its citizens, i.e., as an
element of 'social citizenship'. A right to a minimum income is
therefore not only the corner-stone of a modern system of social
protection, but also of the modern European welfare state.

Within those Member States which provide on principle a right
to minimum resources, a distinction can be made between those
'regimes' in which an unconditional subjective right exists for
everyone; 'general schemes' (e.g. Germany, Netherlands); and those
in which the right to social assistance is only guaranteed to certain
categories of the population under specific conditions and for a
limited period of time – 'categorical schemes' (e.g. France). Other
'regimes' consist of several minimum income or social assistance
schemes: Belgium, Ireland, United Kingdom.

Mere maintenance of subsistence may not guarantee social
inclusion, or may even facilitate social exclusion by stigma, non-
accessibility or by providing the socio-economic minimum without
creating the opportunity to participate in other fields of social life,
especially in the labour market. Therefore, schemes which provide
persons in need with the social minimum, i.e., the necessary means
to meet the essential needs, and promote at the same time
vocational and/or social integration of the needy person, are a new
instrument. Such schemes can be seen in France, Luxembourg,
several autonomous communities in Spain and several local communities in Italy.

The schemes split in responsibilities between central, regional and local government with respect to legislation, administration and financing. In Italy, Portugal and Spain categorical schemes exist at both the national level (non-contributory pensions for the elderly and the disabled) and the local/regional level (minimum income schemes which are linked to integration measures, such as the *renta mínima* in several Spanish *Comunidades Autónomas*).

Schemes also differ in the extent to which they are discretionary or based on a legal right to assistance, which may also mean the existence of an appeal structure. Germany has a very legalised system on the one hand, whereas Denmark, on the other hand, is far less legalised.[22]

Social assistance and welfare regimes

A comparison of the minimum income or social assistance schemes highlights internal differences that produce a different picture to that which is usually seen when the unit of comparison is the totality of the welfare state variation. The most frequently applied distinction of the social policy model is based on the 'residual', 'handmaiden' and 'institutional' models of social policy.[23]

According to the 'residual model', the main sources of welfare ought to be found in the private market and the family. Social welfare should only come into play when these 'natural channels' break down, and then only for a limited time, providing welfare at a minimum level (Peacock: 'the true object of the welfare state is to teach people how to do without it'). The clearest example of welfare according to this model is the Poor Law of nineteenth-century Britain, as well as of other countries.[24] While social assistance is seen as a remnant of this model, we shall argue that the different national schemes also show variations in the degree of residuality.

The 'handmaiden' model (or 'industrial achievement performance model') sees welfare as an adjunct to the economy. Benefits are distributed on the basis of work merit, usually in return for contributions which are fixed as percentages of income from work.

In the 'institutional redistributive model', welfare is seen as a major integrated institution in society, providing universal benefits outside the market on the basis of need.

In a second tradition the focus is on the 'social division of welfare'. The three competing providers of welfare under this tradition are identified as 'private insurance' and the 'workplace' (= occupational welfare), the 'taxation system' (= fiscal welfare) and the 'state' or other public agencies (= social welfare). A fourth category, 'informal welfare' or 'voluntary welfare' should perhaps be added.

Recently a new research tradition has developed.[25] The term 'welfare state regimes' focuses on the clustering of regional welfare traditions covering similar countries. Esping-Andersen's main variable is the extent of decommodification through welfare. It naturally follows that the focus is on social insurance. While this form of welfare can be met through different providers, there is no option for private or occupational welfare for the social assistance clientele. Recipients of social assistance are mostly excluded from work and their need situations are not a natural target for private insurance industry.

As a large and growing proportion of European citizens depend on monetary transfers from the public purse, models must be developed that can help analyse the internal divisions in these systems. By focusing on the relationship between the two main forms of public income maintenance, social insurance and social assistance, the 'institutional-residual' distinction takes on a new dimension and internal cleavages in the regimes become visible.

Esping-Andersen distinguishes between three welfare regimes, where the main criterion is the extent to which the provision of welfare is disconnected from the recipient's position in the economic market, i.e., 'decommodification'.

Welfare in the 'liberal regime' (e.g. the United States, Canada and the United Kingdom, which is increasingly falling within this tradition) is characterised by either means-tested benefits or meagre universal benefits targeted at the working class and the poor. A consequence of this is a strong division between public and private/ occupational welfare.

This contrasts with the more extensive and generous social welfare in the 'conservative/corporatist regime' (e.g. France, Germany). The focus of this regime is mainly on those who are or have been active in the labour force, and the maintenance of status has been given priority over allocation according to need.

In the 'social-democratic regime' (e.g. the Nordic countries), there is a combination of welfare according to need and standard security within social insurance. This represents the model where welfare has achieved the highest degree of decommodification.

In addition to the distribution of income maintenance, welfare can also be seen as a system which imposes *sanctions* on its recipients. The clearest example from history is the internment in the workhouse and the loss of citizens' rights under the Poor Laws. Present social assistance schemes have, albeit to varying degrees, maintained elements of this tradition (see, for instance, Atkinson for the United Kingdom: 'this general means-tested assistance, the modern day version of the Poor Law, is now called "Income Support" ').[26]

The 'internal division of public welfare' becomes central to such a perspective. Hence, a different picture of welfare variation results when the focus is changed from *redistribution* or from the *relationship between private and public welfare providers* to the *relationship between social insurance and social assistance*.

Adding the southern European countries, four poverty regimes in European welfare can be described:

(i) One outcome of the emphasis on poverty in the British 'liberal' regime is that welfare for the poorest and most marginalised groups has developed further away from the liberal doctrines of the Poor Law compared to similar arrangements in other countries. Social insurance is largely limited to serving as an instrument in the fight against poverty and has proved ineffective in securing standard income security for its beneficiaries. The latter is left to the market. As a consequence, public welfare is relatively undivided. This nature of the British assistance scheme justifies the term 'institutionalised poverty regime';

(ii) In the 'corporatist regime' (France, Germany), there is a stronger division between social insurance and social assistance than in the first type. Social assistance is, however, still extensive in coverage, and income maintenance in the form of clear rules of entitlement dominates. Unlike the United Kingdom, however, the continued presence of elderly and disabled people – and recently of the long-term unemployed and single parents – has brought about a division of social assistance in the continental countries. In Germany, for example, the benefits for the elderly and the handicapped are higher than those awarded under the lower-tier general schemes (because of the supplements which are paid to claimants beyond pensionable age – 65 years – under the

Sozialhilfe scheme in the form of aid to subsistence).
Combined, these two forms of social assistance can be
described by the term 'differentiated poverty regime';

(iii) Social assistance in the Nordic 'social-democratic regime'
(Denmark) is marginalised through the extension of social
insurance. The target group is therefore limited to the very
poorest of the able bodied. A strong emphasis on social
control and treatment has resulted from an understanding
that these people are in need of 'something more' than
income maintenance only. In the 'institutional social-
democratic regime' we therefore find a persistent 'residual
poverty regime';

(iv) It is more difficult to identify one southern Europe regime.
Leibfried applies the term 'rudimentary regime'.[27] Great
internal differences give, however, reason to be careful about
grouping together a 'southern rest-category' under one label.

The southern European countries share, however, the feature of
categorical schemes for the disabled. There exists no universal
network of benefits for all persons in need. In this situation, the
absence of general assistance forces large groups to rely on the
family and voluntary organisations for aid. A provisional term to
describe this situation could be 'incomplete differentiated regimes'.

However, recent developments in France, as well as the debate
in the other Latin countries, give reason to expect the emergence
of a new type of poverty regime.[28] When France, as the first Latin
country, introduced a general scheme (RMI), this was seen by the
legislator as an expression of a new solidarity. The emphasis is on
integration in the form of social treatment and control and may
be described by the term 'integration'.

Recommendation on resources and social assistance

The response of the Commission[29] to the patchy and diverse nature
of minimum income guarantee schemes within Member States, was
to propose in 1991 a draft Recommendation for the Council of
Ministers concerning 'common criteria'.[30] The aim behind this
draft, which emerged as a Council Recommendation on 24 June
1992, was to get the Member States to recognise a general right
to a guarantee of sufficient, stable and reliable resources and bene-

fits, and to organise the ways and means of implementing that right.

The *Council Recommendation of 24 June 1992 on Common Criteria Concerning Sufficient Resources and Social Assistance in Social Protection Systems*[31] is that Member States should recognise the basic right of a person to sufficient resources and social assistance in order to be able to live with dignity, and that this should be part of a comprehensive and consistent drive to combat social exclusion. Member States are also recommended to adapt their social protection systems according to common principles and guidelines. The right to sufficient resources and social assistance is to be based on respect for human dignity.

Every person who does not have access individually, or within the household in which he or she lives, to sufficient resources is to have the right to social assistance. However, there may be conditions. Persons will be required to be available for work or vocational training if their age, health and family situation permits. Where appropriate, they may equally have to participate in economic and social integration measures, while persons in full-time employment or students may be legally excluded altogether. For persons who are, in principle, entitled to assistance, access to benefit is not to be subject to time limits. The right may, notwithstanding, be granted for limited but renewable periods. Finally, the right to sufficient resources is additional and subsidiary to other social rights. The implication of this is that parallel efforts should be made to integrate all persons into the general systems of social protection (such as contributory schemes).

The Recommendation states that the amount of resources considered sufficient to cover essential needs is to be fixed taking account of living standards and price levels in the Member States for different types and sizes of household. These basic amounts are to be adjusted or supplemented to meet specific needs. While the Recommendation does not provide a precise methodology for determining the level of resources necessary to cover essential needs, it recommends reference to appropriate indicators, such as, for example, statistical data on the average disposable income in the Member State, or on household consumption. A legal minimum wage, if this exists, or the level of prices, are both points of reference.

The Recommendation is clear that arrangements for periodic review of the levels, based on the indicators, must be established in order to ensure that needs continue to be adequately covered. Persons whose resources (individual or household) are lower than the specified amounts (adjusted or supplemented as appropriate) are entitled to a financial aid equal to the deficiency in their resources.

Moreover, the Recommendation seeks to ensure that regulations in force in other areas of policy, including taxation, civil obligations and social security, all take account of the requirement that individuals should have sufficient resources and social assistance to live in a manner compatible with human dignity. Measures are also to be taken to enable claimants to receive appropriate social support, including information, advice, counselling and assistance in obtaining their rights and, hence, to increasing the level of take-up of benefits. For people whose age and condition render them fit for work, arrangements are to be adopted which will ensure that these persons receive effective help to enter or re-enter working life, including professional training where appropriate. At the same time, an incentive to seek employment must be safeguarded. Administrative procedures and arrangements for assessing means and circumstances are to be as simplified as far as possible, and easily accessible independent appeals systems must be organised.

The measures laid down in this Recommendation are to be progressively implemented from June 1992, with the expectation that a progress report will be drawn up after five years. The economic and budgetary resources in the different Member States, as well as the priorities set by national governments are to be taken into account, all of which may act to slow down progress. However, it is not seen as desirable that the guaranteed minimum initiative should lead to any substantial shift in the balance of social security from social insurance to means testing, though clearly this is a danger. The *Council Recommendation on Convergence of Social Protection Objectives and Policies*[32] includes the need to upgrade them where they are deficient, and is partly intended to ward of this shift to means testing.

Future developments

A major Community concern is that the Single European Market may increase the risk of marginalisation and social exclusion. If this happens, larger numbers of people will be in need of financial support and without any eligibility for other forms of social protection. This will in turn increase the requirement for guaranteed minimum income schemes in the Member States.

However, the case for convergence of guaranteed minimum income schemes is not based solely on these fears, very real though they may be. There are practical, technical and moral reasons as well. For example, convergence of minimum income schemes can serve to counteract migration within the Community, as people are attracted to the Member States with the most generous welfare systems. 'Social tourism' of this kind should be avoided by country-specific minimum income provisions that are consistent with the standard of living and income structure of Member States. While there should be an obligation to grant minimum income benefits to all residents, this should not extend to the 'export' of such benefits since they are financed out of national budgets and reflect the economic and social conditions of each Member State.

The case for convergence of guaranteed minimum income schemes within the Community can also be made on grounds of *social justice*. Any resident within the Community should be provided with access to a minimum subsistence in order to be able to lead a life that is worthy of a human being regardless of such factors as age, sex, race, nationality or professional status. It follows that all Member States should provide a guaranteed minimum income which is the first, and perhaps most important, step towards convergence.

Solidarity is a further reason although, at the Community level, a concern with solidarity is mostly evident in the European Structural Funds. The Regional Fund is designed to encourage job creation and structural adjustments in those parts of the Community which are seriously affected by industrial decline or where development is lagging behind other areas. The main task of the European Social Fund is to promote vocational training or retraining and integration into the labour market of young people and the long-term unemployed. The Single European Act had the effect of doubling the size of the Structural Funds (to about 16 billion ECU in 1993).

The chapter on 'Economic and Social Cohesion' (Articles 130a-1303, EC Treaty), which was included in the EEC Treaty by the Single European Act, demands more solidarity between the 'rich' and the 'poor' Member States, but does not generate any legally binding rights and obligations between Member States to bring about more redistribution. At the summit of Maastricht, however, a specific fund was created which is designed to further socioeconomic cohesion by financial measures.

A guaranteed minimum income common to all Member States could take one of two forms: a basic income or a minimum income guarantee. A basic income is paid to all individual citizens without any test of need and without any reference to their work status. Everyone would receive a monthly payment, with the amount possibly varying with age or disability. In contrast, a minimum income guarantee is designed to bring people up to a certain level and as such is based on a means test, payments only being made to those with resources below a certain level. A minimum income guarantee also requires that people should make efforts to acquire an income of their own. For those below pensionable age who are able to work, there is also a requirement that they be in work or at least be seeking work.

Any form of basic income guarantee would undermine the capacity and relevance of traditional work-oriented, contributory systems of social protection and necessitate a fundamental restructuring of the welfare provisions in Member States. It would be unrealistic, therefore, for the Community to promote a basic income as a universal state guarantee, adequate to meet basic needs.[33]

On the other hand, a minimum income guarantee based on the 'social assistance approach', the subsidiary principle and a means test, seems to be a necessary stage in the evolution of European welfare states. In view of the increased risks arising from the erosion of traditional employment and social protection, such a scheme should be high on the agenda of the European Community. There is a case, therefore, for the Community actively to further the implementation of minimum income and social assistance schemes in the Member States. However, the States and not the Community must be responsible for social policy, in accordance with the distribution of powers within the European Community.[34] In the first instance, therefore, it is up to the Member States to take the necessary steps.[35]

NOTES AND REFERENCES

1 The Challenge of 'New Poverty'

1. Noirot, Paul (ed.) (1993) *Chômage, pauvreté, exclusions* (special edition of *Panoramiques*), Paris, Corlet, p. 126.
2. O'Higgins, M. and S. Jenkins (1989) *Poverty in Europe: Estimates for the Numbers in Poverty in 1975, 1980, 1985,* paper presented to seminar on poverty statistics, Noordwijk, The Netherlands.
3. European Parliament (1993) *Briefing,* 12–16 July, Strasbourg, p. 3.
4. McFate, Katherine (1991) *Poverty, Inequality and the Crisis of Social Policy,* Washington DC, Joint Center for Political and Economic Studies; McFate, Katherine, Roger Lawson and William Julius Wilson (eds) (1995) *Poverty, Inequality and the Future of Social Policy,* New York, Russell Sage.
5. US Bureau of the Census (1988) 'Money Income and Poverty Status in the US' in *Current Population Reports,* Series P-60, Washington DC Government Printing Office.
6. *Listener* (1988) 'Moore's American Cure for Britain's "Dependency" Culture', 18 February.
7. Social Security Committee (1993) *Low Income Statistics: Low Income Families 1979–1989,* London, HMSO.
8. Commission on Social Justice (1993) *The Justice Gap,* London, Institute for Public Policy Research.
9. Esping-Andersen, G. and W. Korpi (1984) 'Social Policy as Class Politics in Post-War Capitalism' in J. H. Goldthorpe (ed.) *Order and Conflict in Contemporary Capitalism,* Oxford, The Clarendon Press.
10. Commission of the European Communities (1992) *Observatory on National Policies to Combat Social Exclusion: Second Annual Report,* Brussels, Ch. 4.
11. Schneider, Ulrich (1993) *Solidarpakt gegen die Schwachen,* München, Knaur, p. 36.
12. Adamy, Wilhelm (1993) 'Sozialhilfeniveau und Arbeitnehmereinkommen', *Soziale Sicherheit,* 42 (6), pp. 161–8.
13. Schneider *Solidarpakt,* Ch. 1.

14. Unicef (1993) *Progress of Nations*.
15. Mack, J. and S. Lansley (1985) *Poor Britain*, London, George Allen and Unwin.
16. Balsen, W. H., H. Nahielski, K. Roessel and R. Winkel (1985) *Die Neue Armut*, Cologne, Bund Verlag.
17. Commission on Social Justice, *The Justice Gap*.
18. Commission of the European Communities (1993) *Occupational Segregation of Men and Women in the European Community*, Brussels.
19. Neckerman, K. R., W. Aponte and W. J. Wilson (1988) 'Family Structure, Black Unemployment and American Social Policy', in M. Weir, A. Orloff and T. Skocpol *The Politics of Social Policy in the United States*, Princeton, Princeton University Press.
20. Wilson, William Julius (1991a) *The Poorest of the Urban Poor: Race, Class and Social Isolation in America's Inner-City Ghettos*, The Eighth T. H. Marshall Memorial Lecture, University of Southampton, England; Wilson, William Julius (1987) *The Truly Disadvantaged: The Inner City, the Underclass and Public Policy*, Chicago, the University of Chicago Press.
21. Rainwater, L. (1991) *Poverty in Americans' Eyes*, Luxembourg Income Study, CEPS/INSEAD, Mimeo.
22. Duster, Troy (1995) *Post-Industrialism and Youth Unemployment: African-Americans as Harbingers*, in McFate, K. R. Lawson and W. J. Wilson (eds) *Poverty, Inequality and the Future of Social Policy* pp. 461–88.
23. Smith, Susan (1989) *The Politics of 'Race' and Residence*, Cambridge, Polity Press, p. 172.
24. Leech, K. and K. Amin (1988) 'A New "Underclass": Race and Poverty in the Inner City', *Poverty*, No.70, CPAG Ltd; Amin, K., with C. Oppenheim, (1992) *Poverty in Black and White: Deprivation and Ethnic Minorities*, London, CPAG and Runneymede Trust.
25. Veenman, J. (1990) *De arbeidsmarktpositie van allochtonen in Nederland, in het bijzonder van Molukkers* (The Labour Market Position of Migrants in the Netherlands with special reference to the Moluccans), Gröningen, Wolters-Noordhoff.
26. Wilson, William Julius (1991b) 'Public Policy Research and the Truly Disadvantaged', in C. Jencks and p. Peterson (eds) *The Urban Underclass*, Washington DC, The Brookings Institute, p. 475.
27. Schmitter-Heisler, B. (1991) A Comparative Perspective on the Underclass', *Theory and Society*, 20, pp. 455–83.
28. Herbert, U. (1991) *A History of Foreign Labour in Germany*, Leamington Spa, Berg.
29. Herbert, U. *A History of Foreign Labour*; Gugel, Gunther (1990) *Ausländer, Aussiedler, Ubersiedler*, Tübingen, Verein für Friedenspädagogik; Wilpert, C. (1991) 'Migration and ethnicity in a non-immi-

gration country: Foreigners in a United Germany', *New Community*, 18 (1); Winkler, Beate (ed.) (1993) *Zukunfstangst Einwanderung*, Munich, Beck.

30. Herbert, U. *A History of Foreign Labour*, p. 250.
31. Freeman, Gary (1986) 'Migration and the Political Economy of the Welfare State', *Annals of the American Academy of Political and Social Sciences*, 485, May, p. 62.
32. Ibid.
33. Vincent, David (1991) *Poor Citizens*, London and New York, Longman.
34. Dean, H. and P. Taylor-Gooby (1993) *Dependency Culture*, London, Harvester Wheatsheaf, pp. 145–6
35. Wilson, William Julius (1991c) 'Studying Inner-City Social Dislocations: The Challenge of Public Agenda Research' *American Sociological Review*, 56 (February), pp. 1–14.
36. Ibid.
37. Lawson, Roger and William Julius Wilson (1995) 'Poverty, Social Rights and the Quality of Citizenship' in McFate, K., R. Lawson and W. J. Wilson (eds) *Poverty*, pp. 693–715.
38. Ashton, D. and Maguire, M. (1991) 'Patterns and Experiences of Unemployment', in P. Brown and R. Scase (eds) *Poor Work: Disadvantage and the Division of Labour*, Milton Keynes and Philadelphia, Open University Press.
39. Townsend, P. et al. (1987) *Poverty and Labour in London*, London Low Pay Unit, p. 52.
40. Ryan, A. (1992) 'The Retreat from Caring', *The Times*, London, 12 August.
41. Standing, Guy (1995) *Labour Insecurity through Market Regulation: Challenge of the 1990s* in K. McFate, R. Lawson and W. J. Wilson (eds) *Poverty*, pp. 153–96; see also Noirot, P. *Chômage*.
42. *Der Spiegel* (1992) 'Jeder Streichelt Seinen Bimbo', January.

2 The Need for a New International Poverty Line

1. Eurostat (1990) *Poverty in Figures: Europe in the Early 1980s*, Luxembourg, p. 23.
2. Atkinson, A. B., K. Gardiner, V. Lechene and H. Sutherland (1993) *Comparing Poverty in France and the United Kingdom*, Suntory-Toyota International Centre for Economics and Related Disciplines, WSP/84, London, London School of Economics.
3. Fisher, G. M. (1992a) 'Poverty Guidelines for 1992', *Social Security Bulletin*, Vol. 55, No. 1; Ruggles, P. (1990) *Drawing the Line: Alterna-*

tive Measures and their Implications for Public Policy, Washington DC, The Urban Institute Press.

4. World Bank (1993a), *Implementing the World Bank's Strategy to Reduce Poverty: Progress and Challenges*, Washington, World Bank.

5. World Bank (1993a) p. 4; World Bank (1990), *World Development Report 1990: Poverty*, Washington, pp. 25–9.

6. World Bank (1993a), p. 4.

7. World Bank (1990).

8. World Bank (1993a), p. iii.

9. World Bank (1993a), p. 6.

10. World Bank (1990), p. 25.

11. Ibid.

12. World Bank (1990), p. 26.

13. Ibid.

14. World Bank (1990) pp. 26–7.

15. UNDP (1993) *Human Development Report 1992*, New York and Oxford, Oxford University Press, p. 225

16. Jazairy, I., M. Alamgir and T. Panuccio (1992) *The State of World Rural Poverty*, Rome and New York, International Fund for Agricultural Development (IFAD), New York University Press.

17. International Institute for Labour Studies (1993) *The Framework of ILO Action Against Poverty*, Geneva, IILS; Franklin, N. N (1967) 'The Concept and Measurement of "Minimum Living Standards" ', *International Labour Relations*, April.

18. Taylor, L. (1992) 'The World Bank and the Environment: The World Development Report, 1992' in UNCTAD, *International Monetary and Financial Issues for the 1990s*, Research Papers for the Group of 24, New York, United Nations.

19. Townsend, P. (1993) *The International Analysis of Poverty*, Milton Keynes, Harvester Wheatsheaf, Ch. 2.

20. US Department of Commerce (1992) *Income, Poverty and Wealth in the United States: A Chart Book* by L. Lamison-White, Current Population Reports, Consumer Income, series P-60, No.179, p. 11.

21. Commission of the European Communities (1991) *Final Report on the Second European Poverty Programme 1985–89*, Luxembourg, Office for the Official Publications of the European Communities, p. 2.

22. Eurostat (1990) *Poverty*, p. 23.

23. Commission of the European Communities (1981) *Final Report from the Commission to the Council on the First Programme of Pilot Schemes and Studies to Combat Poverty*, Brussels, CEC.

24. Commission of the European Communities, *Second European Poverty Programme* p. 2.

25. Townsend, P. (1979) *Poverty in the United Kingdom*, London, Allen Lane and Penguin pp. 247–8.
26. World Bank (1993a), p. ix.
27. Fisher, G. M. (1992c) 'The Development and History of the Poverty Thresholds', *Social Security Bulletin*, Vol. 55, No. 4.
28. Ibid., p. 23.
29. Ibid., pp. 23–6.
30. Townsend, P. *International Analysis*, Ch. 2.
31. World Bank (1993a) p. 27.
32. Ibid., p. 26.
33. Ibid.
34. Ibid., pp. 26–7.
35. Ibid., p. 27.
36. Townsend, P. *Poverty in the UK*, pp. 241–62.
37. Department of Social Security (1993) *Households Below Average Income 1990–1*, London, HMSO.
38. Wolfson, M. C. and Evans J. M. (1989) 'Statistics Canada: Low Income Cut-Offs: Methodological Concerns and Possibilities', Research Paper Series, Statistics Canada, Analytical Studies Branch.
39. Atkinson, Gardiner, Lechene and Sutherland (1993) *Comparing Poverty*; Atkinson, A. B. (1991) *Poverty, Statistics, and Progress in Europe*, Suntory-Toyota International Centre for Economics and Related Disciplines, WSP/60, London, London School of Economics; Atkinson, A. B. (1990a) *A National Minimum? A History of Ambiguity in the Determination of Benefit Scales in Britain*, Suntory-Toyota International Centre for Economics and Related Disciplines, WSP/47, London, London School of Economics.
40. Townsend, P. and D. Gordon (1991) 'What is Enough? New Evidence on Poverty Allowing the Definition of a Minimum Benefit' in Adler, M., C. Bell and A. Sinfield (eds) *The Sociology of Social Security*, Edinburgh, Edinburgh University Press.
41. Townsend, P. *Poverty in the UK*, Ch. 6; Oppenheim, C. (1993) *Poverty: The Facts*, revised and updated edition, London, Child Poverty Action Group.
42. Bradshaw, J. (1993a) *Household Budgets and Living Standards*, York, Joseph Rowntree Foundation; Bradshaw, J. (1993b), *Budget Standards for the United Kingdom*, Aldershot, Avebury/Ashgate Publishing Ltd.
43. Ibid., p. 3.
44. Ibid., p. 6.
45. Ibid.
46. Oldfield, N. and A. C. S. Yu (1993) *The Cost of a Child: Living Standards for the 1990s*, London, Child Poverty Action Group; Piachaud, D. (1979) *The Cost of a Child*, London, Child Poverty Action

Group; Piachaud, D. (1984) *Round About Fifty Hours a Week: The Time Costs of Children*, London, Child Poverty Action Group.

47. Orshansky, M. (1965) 'Counting the Poor: Another Look at the Poverty Profile', *Social Security Bulletin*, Vol. 28, No. 3 and; Fisher, G. M. (1992b) 'The Development of the Orshansky Poverty Thresholds and their Subsequent History as the Official US Poverty Measure', Office of the Assistant Secretary for Planning and Evaluation in the Department of Health and Human Services (unpublished paper); Fisher G. M., *Poverty Thresholds*.

48. Watts, H. W. (1993), 'A Review of Alternative Budget-Based Expenditure Norms', prepared for the panel on poverty measurement of the US Committee on National Statistics, March, Washington DC; Renwick, T. J. and B. Bergmann (1993) 'A Budget-Based Definition of Poverty', *Journal of Human Resources*, Vol. 12, No. 1, pp. 1–24.

49. Bradshaw, J., *Household Budgets*, p. 31.

50. Ibid., p. 30.

51. Mack, J. and S. Lansley (1985) *Poor Britain*, London, George Allen and Unwin.

52. Gordon, D. (ed.) (1994) *Breadline Britain in the 1990s*, York, Joseph Rowntree Foundation.

53. Townsend, P. *The International Analysis of Poverty*; Townsend, P. *Poverty in the UK*.

54. Desai, M. and A. Shah (1985) *An Econometric Approach to the Measurement of Poverty*, Suntory-Toyota International Centre for Economics and Related Disciplines, WSP/2, London, London School of Economics; Desai, M. (1986) 'Drawing the Line: On Defining the Poverty Threshold', in Golding, P. (ed.), *Excluding the Poor*, London, Child Poverty Action Group; Desai M. and A. Shah (1988) 'An Economic Approach to the Measurement of Poverty', *Oxford Economic Papers*, Vol. 40, pp. 505–22; De Vos, K. and A. Hagenaars (1988) 'A Comparison Between the Poverty Concepts of Sen and Townsend', Rotterdam, Erasmus University; Gordon, D. (ed.) (1994) *Breadline Britain in the 1990s*, York, Joseph Rowntree Foundation; Hutton, S. (1989) 'Testing Townsend: Exploring Living Standards Using Secondary Data Analysis', in Baldwin, S., C. Godfrey and C. Propper (eds), *The Quality of Life*, Routledge and Kegan Paul; Hutton, S. (1991) 'Measuring Living Standard Using Existing National Data Sets', *Journal of Social Policy*, Vol. 20, No. 2. Townsend, P and D. Gordon, 'What is Enough?' in Adler, Bell and Sinfield, *The Sociology of Social Security*; Chow, N. W. S. (1982) 'Poverty in an Affluent City; A Report on a Survey of Low-Income Families in Hong Kong', Hong Kong, Department of Social Work, Chinese University of Hong Kong; Bokor, A. (1984) 'Deprivation: Dimensions and Indices',in Andork, R. and T. Kolosi (eds) 'Stratification and Inequality', Budapest, Budapest

Institute for Social Sciences, Townsend, P. *The International Analysis of Poverty.*
55. World Bank (1993a), p. vii
56. World Bank (1993a), p. 26.
57. Ibid.
58. UNDP, *Human Development Report 1993*, p. 225.
59. Commission of the European Communities, *Second European Poverty Programme*, p. 2.
60. Bradshaw, J., *Household Budgets*, p. 3.
61. Townsend, P., *International Analysis of Poverty.*

For further reading

Atkinson, A. B. (1990b) *Comparing Poverty Rates Internationally: Lessons from Recent Studies in OECD Countries*, Suntory-Toyota International Centre for Economics and Related Disciplines, WSP/53, London, London School of Economics.

Atkinson, A. B. and J. Micklewright (1992a) *The Distribution of Income in Eastern Europe*, WSP/72, The Welfare State Programme, Suntory-Toyota International Centre for Economics and Related Disciplines, London, London School of Economics.

Atkinson, A. B. and Micklewright J. (1992b), *Economic Transformation in Eastern Europe and the Distribution of Income*, Cambridge, Cambridge University Press.

Atkinson, A. B. (1993) *What is Happening to the Distribution of Income in the UK?*, Suntory-Toyota International Centre for Economics and Related Disciplines, WSP/87, London, London School of Economics.

Canadian Council on Social Development (1984) *Not Enough: The Meaning and Measurement of Poverty in Canada*, Ottawa, CCSD.

Committee on Ways and Means (1992) *1992 Green Book*, Washington, US Government Printing Office.

Frayman, H. (1991) *Breadline Britain – 1990s, the Findings of the Television Series*, London, LWT and the Joseph Rowntree Foundation.

Hallerod, B. (1993) 'Poverty in Sweden: A New Approach to the Direct Measurement of Consensual Poverty', Department of Sociology, University of Umea and Social Policy Research Centre, New South Wales, University of New South Wales.

Lewis, G. W. and Ulph D. T. (1988) 'Poverty, Inequality and Welfare', *The Economic Journal*, 98.

Lister, R. (1991) 'Concepts of Poverty', *Social Studies Review*, May, pp. 192–5.

Osberg L. (ed.) (1991) *Economic Inequality and Poverty: International Perspectives*, New York and London, Sharpe.

Simpson R. and Walker R. (1993) *Europe: For Richer or Poorer?*, London, Child Poverty Action Group.

Townsend, P. ,'The Repressive Nature and Extent of Poverty in the UK: Predisposing Cause of Crime', Symposium on the Link Between Poverty and Crime, Proceedings of the 11th Annual Conference of the Howard League on 'Poverty and Crime' 8–10 September 1993. Summary in, *Criminal Justice*, the magazine of the Howard League, 11, 4, October.

UK Research and Development Unit (Local Government Centre, (October); University of Warwick (1992) *The Poverty Summit: The Edinburgh Declaration*, an agenda for change prepared by participants in the 'Poverty Summit' held in Edinburgh, 6–8 December 1992.

UNDP (1992) *Human Development Report, 1992*, New York and Oxford, Oxford University Press.

Whiteford P. (1981) 'The Concept of Poverty', *Social Security Journal*, for the Australian Department of Social Security, December.

World Bank (1993b) *World Development Report 1993: Investing in Health*, Washington, Oxford University Press for the World Bank.

3 Women in Poverty

The author would like to thank the participants in the Friedrich Ebert seminar for their useful comments on the first draft of this chapter.

1. Glendinning, C. and J. Millar (1987) *Women and Poverty in Britain*, Brighton, Harvester Wheatsheaf, p. 3.
2. Lewis, J. and D. Piachaud (1992) 'Women and Poverty in the Twentieth Century' in C. Glendinning and J. Millar (eds) *Women and Poverty in Britain, the 1990s*, Hemel Hempstead, Harvester Wheatsheaf, 1992, p. 27.
3. Oppenheim, C. (1993) *Poverty: The Facts*, London, CPAG.
4. Lister, R. (1992) *Women's Economic Dependency and Social Security*, Manchester, Equal Opportunities Commission.
5. Webb, S. (1993) 'Women and the UK Income Distribution: Past, Present and Prospects', *Fiscal Studies*, Vol. 14, No. 4, November.
6. Whitting, G. (1992) 'Women and Poverty: The European Context' in C. Glendinning and J. Millar (eds) (1992), *Women and Poverty in Britain*.
7. Maruani, M. (1992) 'The Position of Women in the Labour Market' *Women of Europe* No.36, Brussels, Commission of the European Communities, 1992.
8. See for instance Evandrou, M. (1990) *Challenging the Invisibility of Carers: Mapping Informal Care Nationally*, London, STICERD, 1990; Glendinning, C. (1992) *The Costs of Informal Care: Looking Inside*

the Household, London, SPRU/HMSO; McLaughlin, E. (1991) *Social Security and Community Care: The Case of the Invalid Care Allowance,* London DSS/HMSO.

9. See for instance Morris, J. (1991) *Pride Against Prejudice: Transforming Attitudes to Disability,* London, The Women's Press.

10. *Final Report on the Second European Poverty Programme,* Com (91) 29, Brussels, CEC, 1991.

11. Bradshaw, J. and J. Millar (1991) *Lone Parent Families in the UK,* London, DSS/HMSO.

12. Morris, J., *Pride Against Prejudice.*

13. Bradshaw, J. and D. Mitchell (1991) *Lone Parents and their Incomes: A Comparative Study of Ten Countries,* York, University of York. See also Roll, J. (1992) *Lone Parent Families in the European Community,* London, European Family and Social Policy Unit.

14. Meulders, D., C. Hecq and R. Plasman (1992) 'An Assessment of European Evidence on the Employment of Women in 1992' in R. M. Lindley (ed.) *Women's Employment: Britain in the Single European Market,* London, EOC/HMSO.

15. Pillinger, J. (1991) *Feminising the Market – the Single European Market and Women's Employment,* Sheffield, Sheffield Centre for Regional Economic and Social Research.

16. Land, H. (1992) 'A Damaging Dichotomy: Women and Part-time vs Full-time Employment' *Benefits,* No. 5, September/October.

17. Low Pay Unit (1991) *The New Review,* No. 8.

18. The lower female unemployment rate in the UK is, in part, a construct of the method of counting the unemployed which is based on benefit recipients. It also reflects the growth of part-time jobs available to women.

19. Pillinger, J., *Feminising the Market.*

20. Whitting, G., *Women and Poverty.*

21. Glendinning, C. and J. Millar (1987) *Women and Poverty in Britain.*

22. Lister, R., *Women's Economic Dependency.*

23. See Ward, C., H. Joshi and A. Dale (1993) *Income Dependency within Couples,* London, City University; Vogler, C. (1989) *Labour Market Change and Patterns of Financial Allocation within Households* Oxford, Nuffield College; Morris, L. (1990) *The Workings of the Household,* Cambridge, Polity Press; Vogler, C. and J Pahl (1993) 'Social and Economic Change and the Organisation of Money within Marriage', *Work, Employment and Society* Vol. 7, No. 1, March.

24. Lister, R., *Women's Economic Dependency.*

25. Lister, R. (1990) 'Women, Economic Dependency and Citizenship', *Journal of Social Policy,* Vol. 19, No. 4, pp 445–67 and *The Exclusive Society: Citizenship and the Poor,* London, CPAG.

26. Atkinson, A. B. (1991) *Poverty, Statistics and Progress in Europe*, London, STICERD, p. 10.
27. This point has been well made by Stephen Jenkins (1991) 'Poverty Measurement and the Within-household Distribution: Agenda for Action', *Journal of Social Policy*, Vol. 20, pt 4.
28. For a summary, see Lister, *Women's Economic Dependency*.
29. Vogler, *Labour Market Change*.
30. Payne, S. (1991) *Women, Health and Poverty*, Hemel Hempstead, Harvester Wheatsheaf, p. 153. See also Graham, H. (1993) *Hardship and Health in Women's Lives*, Hemel Hempstead, Harvester Wheatsheaf.
31. Kempeneers, M. and E. Lelievre (1990) 'Family and Employment within the Twelve' *Eurobarometer* No. 34, Brussels, Commission of the European Communities.
32. Puttnam, R. D. (1993) 'The Prosperous Community: Social Capital and Public Life' *The American Prospect*, Spring.
33. Pollack, A. (ed.) (1993) *A Citizen's Enquiry: The Opsahl Report on Northern Ireland* , Dublin, Lilliput Press.
34. Stone, D. (1986) 'Stormy Weather: Women and Poverty', *Poverty*, No.6 3, Spring.
35. Dunn, M. (1988) 'Strength in Numbers: The Story of Cowgate's Credit Union', *Poverty*, Spring.
36. Hyatt, S. (1992) 'Accidental Activists: Women and Politics on a Council Estate', *Crosscurrents*, 5, Autumn, p. 93–102.
37. Cook, J. and S. Watt (1992) 'Racism, Women and Poverty' in C. Glendinning and J. Millar, *Women and Poverty in Britain*.
38. Brocas, A., A. Cailloux and V. Ogel (1990) *Women and Social Security: Progress Towards Equality of Treatment*, Geneva, International Labour Office, p. 79.
39. For a discussion of this dilemma see R. Lister (1994) ' "She Has Other Duties" – Women, Citizenship and Social Security' in S. Baldwin and J. Falkingham (eds), *Social Security and Social Change: New Challenges to the Beveridge Model*, Hemel Hempstead, Harvester Wheatsheaf.
40. See Lister, R., *Women's Economic Dependency*; Duncan, A., C. Giles and S. Webb (1994) *Social Security Reform and Women's Independent Incomes*, Manchester, Equal Opportunities Commission.
41. See Lister, R., *Women's Economic Dependency*; Commision on Social Justice (1994) *Social Justice: Strategies for National Renewal*, London, Vintage.

4 Poverty, Instability and Minimum Income for Integration (RMI) in France

1. Revenu Minimum d'Insertion
2. 1,160,000 beneficiaries
3. 520,000 beneficiaries
4. Amounts increased to F2,325.66 in 1995 for a single person, plus F1,162.83 for the second person and F697.69 for each extra person or child; this sum is increased to F930.26 from the third child.
5. A specific right had been provided for in the law of 1988 to give entitlement to housing benefit: this was made universal from 1990 to 1992 for the whole of the population, resulting in a kind of positive discrimination. The maximum rate is granted, since income is considered as nil, even when it is not.
6. The actual net charge is significantly lower. In fact initially the rate of 20 per cent was calculated to 'recycle' the average saving to the General Councils because of the establishment of the RMI (savings in respect of social aid to infants, local low-income complements, etc.). Today, given the big increase in the guaranteed minimum income, the average net cost for General Councils can be estimated at approximately 50 per cent.
7. Excluding government departments.
8. A priest in Paris who called for public buildings to be used to house the homeless during the winter.
9. As authorised by the law of 29 July 1992 this represents approximately half of the gross cost; this limit is justified by the previous costings for legal medical assistance for expenditure for care.
10. Cf. report of the 'Economic Outlook' of the Commissariat General of the Plan, July 1994.
11. Job applications (cat.1) in CVS figures, October 1994. Source: DARES.

5 Unemployment, the Threat of Poverty, and Social Security in Germany

1. Lawson, Roger (1993) *The Challenge of 'New Poverty': Lessons from Europe and North America*, Friedrich Ebert Foundation Euroseminar.
2. *Hamburger Abendblatt* (1994) 11 January.
3. Federal Office of Statistics (1993) *Sozialhilfe 1991*, Wiesbaden.
4. Hanesch, W. (1994) *Armut in Deutschland*, Reinbek, p. 182.
5. Ibid., p. 142ff.
6. Schäfer, C. (1993) *'Armut' und 'Reichum' sind die Verteilungspolitischen Aufgaben* in WSI-Mitteilungen, p. 617ff.

7. See the 'Bremen Surveys' e.g. Leisering, L., W. Voges, 'Erzeugt der Wohlfahrtsstaat seine eigene Klientel?' in S. Liebfried, W. Voges (1992) *Armut im Wohlfahrtstaat*, special edition of *Kölner Zeitschrift für Sozialogie und Sozialpsychologie*, Opladen, pp. 446ff, and further references.
8. Krause, P., *Zur Zeitlichen Dimension der Einkommensarmut* in W. Hanesch, *Armut in Deutschland*, pp. 198ff.
9. Schäfer, C., *'Armut' und 'Reichum'*.
10. OECD-Statistics 1992 in *Die Zeit* 19 November 1993.

6 A New Social Policy for the 'Active Society'

1. Employment in Europe Conference, Brussels, 19–21 October 1993.
2. Commission of the European Communities (1993) 'European Social Policy: Options for the Union', Green Paper, Brussels, November, p. 16.
3. Eurostat (1990) 'Inequality and Poverty in Europe 1980–5', Brussels; Low Pay Unit (1993) 'Poor Excuses', *New Review*, No. 23, London, August/September.
4. Pond, Chris and Jennie Popay (1993) 'Poverty, Economic Inequality and Health', in *Dilemmas in Health Care*, Milton Keynes, Open University.
5. Townsend, Peter (1993) *The International Analysis of Poverty*, Milton Keynes, Harvester Wheatsheaf.
6. Central Statistical Office (1993) *Economic Trends*, London, HMSO.
7. Pond, Chris (1993) 'Budgetary Engineering: Taxes, Transfers and Incentives for Jobs', paper to the EC Employment in Europe Conference, Brussels.
8. Commission of the European Communities 'European Social Policy', Green Paper, Brussels, November, p. 14.
9. Churchill, Winston (1909) *Liberalism and the Social Problem*, London, Hodder and Stoughton.
10. Macmillan, Rt Hon. Harold (1946) 'Official Report', London, House of Commons.
11. Commission of the European Communities (1993) *Employment in Europe 1993*, Brussels, p. 99.
12. Quoted in Commission of European Communities (1992) *Combating Social Exclusion: Fostering Integration*, Report of a Conference, Brussels, 2–3 April.
13. Townsend, Peter (1993) 'Hard Times: What Hopes for European Social Policy?' in Coates and Barratt Brown (eds) (1993) *A European Recovery Programme*, Nottingham, Spokesman Books.

14. Coates, Ken and Michael Barratt Brown (eds) *A European Recovery Programme*.

7 New Policies for the Twenty-first Century

1. See Schulte, B. 'Social Security Legislation in the European Communities: Co-ordination, Harmonisation and Convergence', in Dieters, D. (ed.) (1991) *Social Security in Europe*, Brussels, Bruylant, pp. 153–75.
2. For more recent scenarios (the 'thirteenth state', the 'social snake') see Dieters, D. 'Will 1992 lead to the Co-ordination and Harmonisation of Social Security?', in idem (ed.) *Social Security in Europe* (note 1), pp. 177–90 (with references).
3. For further details see Commission of the EC (1990) Community Charter of Basic Social Rights for Workers and the Action Programme relating to the implementation of the Charter in *Social Europe* 1, pp. 45–50 and 51–76.
4. Ibid.
5. Council of the EC (1992) Recommendation by the Council on convergence of social protection objectives and policies (92/441/EEC), Official Journal No.L 945/49, 26 August.
6. For more details see Commission of the EC (1992) 'Social Security for persons moving within the Community', *Social Europe*, 3.
7. See Henningsen, B. (1991/2) 'Die Schönste Nebensache Europas. Zur Geschichte der EG-Sozialpolitik', in *Sozialer Fortschritt* (5F) 41, pp. 203–12.
8. For the legislative framework for this see vast case-law of the European Court of Justice and, most recently: *Equality of Treatment between Women and Men in Social Security*, A European Conference at Lincoln College, University of Oxford 4–6 January 1994 (documentation forthcoming).
9. Carton, B. (1992) 'Introduction to the European Community "Poverty 3" Programme' in Europe, *Colloquy Towards Greater Social Justice in Europe: The Challenge of Marginalisation and Poverty*, Strasbourg, 3–5 December 1991, Proceedings of the Council of Europe, pp. 48–50.
10. For further details see Commission of the European Communities (1981) *Final Report of the First Programme to Combat Poverty*, Brussels, EC.
11. See Townsend, P. (1979) *Poverty in the United Kingdom*, Harmondsworth, Penguin.
12. Commission of the European Communities, National Policies to Combat Social Exclusion (1991) First Annual Report of the European Community Observatory, Brussels, EC.
13. *Social Europe Supplement* 2/89.

14. Commission of the European Communities (1991) *Final Report on the Second European Poverty Programme (1985–9)*, COM (91) 29 Final, Brussels.

15. For further details see Commission of the European Communities (1993) *Final Report on the Community Programme on the Economic and Social Integration of the Least Privileged Groups (1989–94)*, COM (93) 435 Final, Brussels ('Poverty 3').

16. COM (89) 568 Final, Brussels, 29 November 1989.

17. See section in text on the Convergence of Social Security Objectives within the Community pp. 122.

18. See Commission of the EC/MISSOC (1991) *Social Protection in the Member States of the Community: Situation on 1 July 1991 and evolution*, Leuven, EEC/MISSOC. This volume offers, by means of comparative tables, a comparison of social protection schemes in the 12 Member States.

19. See Commission of the EC (1993), *Social Protection in Europe*, Brussels, p. 42.

20. See Schulte, B. 'Guaranteed Minimum Resources and the European Community' in Simpson, R., Walker, R. *et al.* (1993) *Europe for Richer or Poorer?*, London, Child Poverty Action Group, pp. 39–51.

21. For these details see Lodemel, I., Schulte, B. (1992) 'Social Assistance – A Part of Social Security or the Poor Law in New Disguise?' in *European Institute of Social Security Yearbook*, EISS (1993) 'Reforms in Eastern and Central Europe', Leuven, Acco, pp. 515–43; and paper presented at the conference 'Social Security 50 Years after Beveridge', York 27–30 September 1992.

22. For further details see Schulte, B. (1991) 'Das Recht auf ein Mindesteinkommen in der Europäischen Gemeinschaft – Nationaler Status Quo und Supranationale Initiativen' in *Sozialer Fortschritt* (SF), pp. 7–23; idem, 'Die Folgen der EG-Integration für die wohlfahrtsstaatlichen Regimes', in *Zeitschrift für Sozialreform (ZSR)*, pp. 548–79; idem (1992) 'Armut und Armutsbekämpfung in der Europäischen Gemeinschaft Mindesteinkommenssicherung und Sozialhilfe in EG-Sozialrecht und EG-Sozialpolitik', in *Zeitschrift für Sozialhilfe und Sozialgesetzbuch* (ZfSH/SGB) 31, pp. 393–402 and pp. 462–72. For further comparative details see Lodemel, I., Schulte, B., 'A Part of Social Security or the Poor Law in New Disguise?' in *Social Security: 50 Years after Beveridge*, Vol. 2: *Competing Models of Social Security: A Comparative Perspective*, York: University of York (conference paper); see also 29 below.

23. See Titmuss, R. (1974) *Social Policy: An Introduction*, London, George Allen and Unwin, pp. 30–1.

24. See Titmuss, R. (1963) *Essays on the Welfare State*, London, George Allen and Unwin, 1963.

25. See Esping-Andersen, G. (1990) *The Three Worlds of Welfare Capitalism*, Cambridge, Polity Press.
26. Atkinson, A., 'The Development of State Pensions in the United Kingdom' in Schmähl, W. (ed.) (1992), *The Future of Basic and Supplementary Pension Schemes in the European Community – 1992 and Beyond*, Baden-Baden, Nomos, 1991, pp. 117–34.
27. Leibfried, S., 'Income Transfer and Poverty Policy in the EC Perspective: On Europe's Slipping into Anglo-American Welfare Models', paper presented at the European Conference on 'Poverty, Marginalisation and Social Exclusion in the Europe of the 90s', Alghero, Italy, 23–5 April 1990.
28. See section in text on Integration of the Least Privileged, p. 129.
29. See for details Schulte, 'Guaranteed Minimum Resources', pp. 45–7.
30. 'Draft Recommendation by the Council on Common Criteria Concerning Sufficient Resources and Social Assistance in the Social Protection Systems', COM (91) 228 Final, 27 June 1991; OJC 194, 25. 7, 1991 p. 13.
31. 92/442/EEC, Official Journal No. L 245/46, 26 August 1992.
32. See above 1.2 and note 5.
33. See for further arguments Schulte, B., 'Minimum Income Strategies', paper presented at the European Conference on Basic Incomes, 15–17 November 1989, Cumberland Lodge, England. Sponsored by the Commission of the European Communities, organised by Deo Ramprakash/Graham Room, University of Bath.
34. 'Poverty Regimes in the USA and the "USE" – Current European Poverty Regimes', paper presented at the Research Conference on Social Policy, the European Community and the United States, Center of European Studies, Harvard University, 1991 (forthcoming).
35. See Commission of the EC (1993) 'European Social Policy. Options for the Union', *Green Book*, Brussels.

INDEX